# Are You Running On Empty?

*Did your doctor tell you about the four gauges that are essential for maintaining good health?*

- ✔ energy
- ✔ pH
- ✔ free radicals
- ✔ inflammation

*Do you know how to correct an imbalance in any of your four gauges?*

# Contents

# Acknowledgments

There are so many people I would like to thank for their help in writing this book. At the top of the list is my wife Rose-Marie who has been my best friend for the last 33 years. Rose-Marie helped me stay focused and was a constant encourager. "Mom" as I like to call her worked tirelessly to help me bring the concept of the book to reality.

# Foreword

It is a privilege to write the foreword for Anthony Martin's new book "Medical Crisis: Secrets Your Doctor Won't Share With You".

This book may literally save or add years to your life. I believe the four warning gauges that Dr. Martin refers to in his book helped extend the life of my wife Gloria, as well as my own. My wife and I sought Dr. Martin's help several years ago. At that time Gloria and I were both in a state of ill health. Personally, I had Chronic Fatigue Syndrome and could hardly engage in practice. My wife was exhausted all the time and the doctors could not find the reason, never mind the solution.

Dr. Martin showed us how to restore our health by following the guidelines found in this book. Today, both Gloria and I are in very good health. We both have great energy and we are truly blessed. We count Dr. Martin and his dear wife Rosie as great friends.

Dr. Martin has been a mentor of ours for years and you will see from this book that he is a master health motivator. You'll find that this book will take you to a new level of health and wellness!! Most importantly, it may be the missing ingredient to help you recover from ill health.

**Dr. Johnny Clubb, B.A., D.C., Msc., RNCP**

# Preface

The other day I was driving my truck and thinking about the things that I had to do. Suddenly, a siren-like alarm went off on the dash of the truck. At first it startled me. Then after I gained my composure I saw a flashing dash board light. It stated "Your fuel is low, Your fuel is low." Wow, it almost made me drive off the road. I must admit that I was impressed. I like the idea of being warned. I appreciate early warnings.

> In the months following the devastating Asian tsunami of December 2004, an amazing story was unfolding from Simuelua Island, the closest inhabited land to the epicenter of the earthquake. A news report said only 7 of the 75,000 inhabitants of the island died when 30 foot waves struck just a half hour after the quake. For decades these islanders had heard stories told by their grandparents of giant waves that killed thousands on the same island in 1907. So when the ground shook and the sea retreated from shore, the people recalled their grandparents warning and fled to high ground. *A warning heeded is a disaster avoided.* (Our Daily Bread, May 3, 2006)

What I am going to share with you in this book is known by the medical field, but rarely used. Here is why. Doctors are highly trained in the treatment of diseases but poorly trained in the prevention of disease. Now I know that traditional medicine would say "Hey! Wait a minute! We prevent heart disease by treating cholesterol. Oh yeah? What do you do with the 50% of heart attack victims that have no cholesterol issues at all? Friends, I have been in the medical field for thirty two years. It is only recently that traditional medicine has begun to emphasize the importance of food and good nutrition in cancer and cardiovascular prevention.

# Introduction

I have discovered *four* early warning detectors. If you listen and watch for them, they will help detect cancer or cardiovascular diseases.

Even without symptoms present, I will mention tests to determine if you are susceptible or have a possible cancer or cardiovascular problem.

Could you imagine what it will be like to have a flashing red light go off inside your head let's say 5 to 10 years before one would get cancer or a heart attack telling you to "check your engine", "you are too low on energy", "your body's pH is too acidic", "your inflammatory response is on *red alert*", or "your free radicals are multiplying too rapidly." Now you can have an early warning system and even more, you can know what to do about it.

I find it ironic that in the USA there are daily terror alert warnings – elevated or extreme danger (orange or amber alert) – yet we have devised very little early warning detection in our bodies – *until now!*

That's right. Now we can have an early warning system. Friends, if you listen to your body and do these simple tests, you will know what your health status truly is. Even more, you will know what to do about it. This book is a *must read* as it can literally *change your life*!

Due to my years of research, I have come to understand that the human body has a truly amazing early warning system. I believe this early warning system will revolutionize preventative medicine. If you follow the advice that I am about to give you and do the four simple tests you will find out if your body is heading for disaster, before you have any major symptoms. Medicine tends, in general, to be disease oriented. When you have a disease, medicine will usually start the cycle of tests and treatment to help you feel better. In my opinion, where medicine has failed, is in the area of true prevention.

I have connected the dots. Your body has *four gauges* that will tell you if something is going wrong. Every traditional and complimentary medical practitioner knows of these gauges. Regrettably, they have not understood their true significance. They may have talked about one or perhaps two of these gauges, but have never put all four of them together. To have an accurate reading of what your body's status is *you need to check all four of these gauges.*

"There is a major communication gap between the scientist and the layman, in that the former is not interested in anything that is "unscientific", while the layman doesn't care how "scientific" the cure is – as long as it works." (Ronald W. Pero Ph.D, Professor – Department of Cell and Molecular Biology – Reverse Aging, Lund University, Sweden)

# Ball Point Pen

Take out a ball point pen. Take a look at the tip. How long do you think it takes for cancer to grow to the size of the tip of the ball point pen? Guess. How many of you said over 5 years? *That's right over 5 years!* People have the idea that cancer cell development occurs overnight. You may think that one day you don't have cancer and the next day you wake up and feel a little lump in your breast and presto you have cancer. Early detection is not waiting until you can feel a lump, or waiting for prostate blood results (elevated PSA). This is not early detection! The cancer has been in your body for years.

## By the time that most cancers are diagnosed they have been in your body for several years.

As you read this book, you will come to understand that these four body status indicators are truly connected. You will see the importance of the body's inflammatory response and how it coincides with the increase in *free radical damage*, the *lowering of the body's pH* and how it *causes one to have low energy levels.*

**Traditional medicine says:** Most disease is caused by germs – kill the microbes – kill whatever is making you sick. Drugs, antibiotics, chemotherapy, radiation, surgery.

**Alternative healing says:** Disease is brought about by imbalance. It's primarily a nutritional, electrical, structural, toxilogical or biological equation. To get well, re-establish balance in the body. Work with it, not against it. (Blood: The River of Life, BioMedx.com)

# Part 1

# THE PROBLEM

## Did You Know?

# In this book I will give answers to the following 60 questions:

## Cancer and Heart:

1. Did you know that breast cancer is *nearly 100% preventable?*

2. Did you know that prostate cancer is *nearly 100% preventable?*

3. Did you know that *almost every heart attack could and should be preventable?*

4. Did you know that *inflammation in your body is responsible for 30% of all cancers?*

5. Did you know that *you get brand new blood every four months?*

6. Did you know that it takes almost *6 to 10 years* for most cancers to grow to the size of the tip of a ball point pen?

## Home:

7. Did you know that just *living in your home could be causing you to be seriously ill?*

8. Did know that household cleaners like *Javex, Chlorox, and Tide may be making you sick?*

9. Did you know that *deodorant and shampoo* can be hazardous to your health?

10. Did you know that living in a *newer home* could be compromising your health?

11. Did you know that *carpets* are the most dangerous form of flooring for your health?

12. Did you know that *air conditioning* in your car, home, office is really dangerous to your health?

13. Did you know that there have been *85,000 new chemicals developed since World War 11?* Many of them are found in your home!

14. Did you know that the average person spends *about 90% of their time indoors?*

15. Did you know that *there are non-toxic cleaners available?*


## Tests:

16. Did you know that your body has *four gauges* that will tell you years ahead of time whether or not you are getting sick?

17. Did you know that most doctors *do not do four routine tests* that could save your life?

18. Did you know that there is a *simple urinary test that will tell you how fast your body is aging?*

19. Did you know that *a simple and inexpensive blood test can tell you up to 8 years before whether or not you will have a heart attack?*

20. Did you know that *measuring your waist* is far more important than any other measurement including BMI (body mass index) *for predicting heart attacks and cancer?*

## Doctors:

21. Did you know that *the number one reason people visit their doctors is for fatigue?*

22. Did you know that *the number one reason that people are so exhausted today is from stress?*

23. Did you know that *95% of all doctors do not use live blood cell analysis?*

24. Did you know that *most doctors never check the pH level of your body fluids?*

## Nutrition:

25. Did you know that we consume *between 120–150 pounds of sugar a year?*

26. Did you know that *sugar depletes your immune system?*

27. Did you know that sugar *slows down* white blood cell activity?

28. Did you know that *hypoglycemia – low blood sugar – is an epidemic in America today?*

29. Did you know that *diabetes is an epidemic in America today?*

30. Did you know that *obesity is an epidemic in America today?*

31. Did you know that *most Americans do not eat enough fiber?*

32. Did you know that we are supposed to *eat 30-40 grams of fiber a day and the average American eats around 10 grams a day?*

33. Did you know that *eating an apple a day* will keep the doctor away?

34. Did you know that *eating a banana* can reduce your chocolate craving?

35. Did you know that it only takes *21 days to form a new habit?*

36. Did you know that there are up to *10 teaspoons of sugar in most sodas?*

37. Did you know that *drinking diet soda is hazardous to your health?*

38. Did you know that you *should never stop completely eating junk food?*

39. Did you know that *most people on a diet don't lose weight because they don't eat enough?*

40. Did you know that *you can eat fruit and vegetables all day long and never gain a pound?*

41. Did you know that *it only takes two days to lose up to 5 pounds of fat?*

42. Did you know that *drinking cow's milk could lead to diabetes?*

43. Did you know that *drinking cow's milk will not prevent osteoporosis?*

44. Did you know that *only 26% of the population eat enough fruits and vegetables every day?*

## Asthma & Children:

45. Did you know that the *overuse of antibiotics* is one of the main reasons there is an asthma epidemic today?

46. Did you know that incidence of *childhood asthma is up 400%?*

47. Did you know that *asthmatic patients often suffer with hypoglycemia (low blood sugar)?*

48. Did you know that *giving antibiotics to babies before they are one year old will make them 2 times more likely to develop asthma?*

## Sleep:

49. Did you know that *over half* of the population in America suffer from sleep disorders?

50. Did you know that having a *green light* on your alarm clock, instead of red, can disturb your sleep?

51. Did you know that *your immune system works much better when you are asleep* then when you are awake?

52. Did you know that *getting exposure to the sunlight will help you sleep better at night?*

## Yeast:

53. Did you know that if you were on *antibiotics* in the last two years you will almost certainly *have developed leaky gut syndrome* and have a *yeast infection* in your blood?

54. Did you know that if you are on the *birth control pill* you probably *have developed leaky gut syndrome* and have a *yeast infection* in your blood?

## Free Radicals:

55. Did you know that the same *oxygen* that you cannot live without is the same oxygen that *will shorten your life span if not controlled?*

56. Did you know that A*lzheimer's disease has a major connection to inflammatory diseases like rheumatic fever and tuberculosis?*

## pH:

57. Did you know that it is *nearly impossible* for someone to get cancer if their pH is alkaline?

58. Did you know that every fruit and every vegetable *helps to make your body fluids' pH more alkaline?*

59. Did you know that it is *almost impossible* to lose weight if your body's fluids are acidic?

## Inflammation:

60. Did you know that if you are *constantly tired* that you have inflammation in your body?

# Chapter 1

# WARNING SYSTEM GAUGE #1

*Energy*

*One way that your body* tries to get your attention and warn you that something in your body is not right is a decrease in energy level. I always ask my patients when they come into my office this question. "Subjectively, if 10 is high and 1 is low where has your energy level generally been in the last several months?" If they say anything less than 8 out of 10 then I explain to them that this is not within normal limits. Not only are they not firing on all cylinders but their body is actually trying to tell them that something is amiss. Friends, if you are not consistently firing on all cylinders and are less than 10 out of 10 for energy on most days, the light, like on your car's dash, is flashing, saying: Check the engine!! Check the engine!!

A general lack of energy by North Americans is at an epidemic stage. The magazine "First – For Women On The Go", since the summer of 2005, has had on the front page every month: "Feeling Foggy and Fatigued? – The Tiredness Cure", "Wired and Tired? – 101 Ways to Get Endless Energy", "Feel Tired Every Day?" People are tired and are obsessed with finding out the reason for their physical weariness.

## A general lack of energy by North Americans is at a epidemic stage.

I think that at this stage it is important to remind you where energy comes from in the first place. The fuel needed for that body of yours comes from the food that you eat. Your body's digestive system is a complex manufacturing plant. (Anybody who does not believe that there is a God after studying the human body has literally kissed their brains goodbye or put it on auto-pilot.) This complex manufacturing plant knows how to take your food that you have just eaten – like fat, protein, carbohydrates, vitamins and minerals and break them down into energy that the body needs. Once these microscopic sized nutrients are assimilated into the bloodstream they are transported by your red blood cells. What does the Bible say? "The life of the flesh is in the blood" (Genesis 9:4). That is absolutely true.

## Blood Cells: Internal Mailmen

Red blood cells deliver essential nutrients to every cell in your body, including brain cells, heart cells, muscle cells etc. These in turn help the body function. Red blood cells are like your internal mailmen. Inside of each and every one of your red blood cells there is an eveready battery called the mitochondria that is supposed to keep you going and going. This mitochondria takes these nutrients and uses them up for energy. If your digestive system is not break-ing down foods properly, *your red blood cells are not absorbing nor delivering nutrients adequately.*

## Tests To Determine Energy Levels: Live Blood Cell Analysis

Live blood cell analysis is a screening test for blood using a specialized darkfield, phase contrast and brightfield microscope. Using the microscope in this way we can evaluate the shapes and properties of individual blood cells thus allowing a multitude of nutritional deficiencies and disorders to be detected. By using this form of testing, problems can be discovered in the early stages of development and preventative measures initiated.

Live blood cell analysis involves taking a single drop of blood from a fingertip prick and magnifying it immediately up to 1,500 times or more under a microscope. This detects if your body is imbalanced. The diseases themselves cannot be seen under the microscope but blood patterns, red blood cell shapes and changes compared to the normal cell shape can be observed before being picked up in a routine laboratory medical blood test.

Traditional medical blood testing involves taking several vials of blood, preserving and sending them to a laboratory for an "autopsy". At the laboratory the preserved blood is analyzed, cells are counted and compared to the normal.

### Ideal Live Microscopic Blood Cell Analysis:

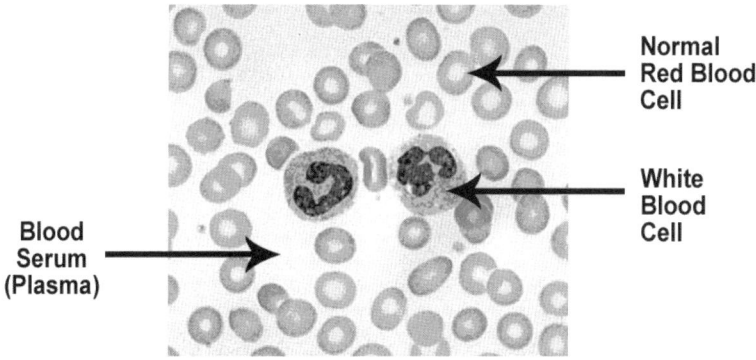

What can a live blood cell analysis detect?

✓ Inconsistences in the red blood cells can indicate nutritional deficiencies.

- ✓ Low levels of iron, protein, vitamin B12, folic acid and fatty acids.

- ✓ Incomplete or delayed digestion of fats and proteins can be seen.

- ✓ Liver stress and undesirable bacterial fungal life form can be detected.

- ✓ Yeast and quantity of yeast can be discovered.

- ✓ Parasites and hormonal imbalances can be ascertained.

## Normal Blood Cells

The *red blood cells* are normally uniform in size and shape and are generally round. They reside freely and are free floating in the blood serum, not overlapping or sticking together, but gently bouncing off each other. Problems start when the shape of the red blood cell changes. It takes 20 seconds for a red blood cell to circulate throughout the whole body. *A single drop of blood contains up to 5 million red blood cells.* Red blood cells live for an average of 120 days and will make 250,000 round trips throughout the body before dying. Eight to ten million red blood cells die each second, and eight to ten million red blood cells are produced every second.

**There are up to 30 trillion red blood cells that are responsible to feed 60 trillion body cells (heart cells, liver cells, kidney cells, brain cells etc.)**

The *white blood cells* are about as large as two red blood cells. These white blood cells have a grainy appearance and have 3 to 4 dark, irregular shaped lobes inside the cell. Rather than being round, they display many different shapes and are active and moving. In normal blood there are 700 to 1000 red blood cells to every white blood cell. White blood cells live from a few days to a few weeks. Bone marrow and lymphatic tissue produce 1 million white blood cells every second.

There can be up to *300,000 platelets* seen in a drop of blood. Platelets are produced in the bone marrow and help prevent blood loss. If you cut your finger, platelets are stimulated to go to the site of injury and form a "plug" to help reduce blood loss. Platelets are free floating and if they start clumping together triglyceride levels could be increasing.

The *blood serum (plasma)* surrounding the cells should be clear without parasitic forms, bacteria, clots or other undesired floating masses. The more waste products seen in the blood serum, the more toxic the patient.

## More Facts Concerning Blood

☞ 90% of blood serum (plasma) is water.

☞ 10% of blood serum is nutrients, glucose, vitamins, and cell waste.

☞ An average person has 5-6 liters of blood.

☞ Arteries carry blood away from the heart.

☞ Veins carry blood back to the heart.

☞ Capillaries connect small arteries to small veins.

**An average person has 100,000 kilometers of blood vessels. Laid end to end they would circle the earth two and a half times.**

## Abnormal Blood Cells

It is normal for the red blood cells to "clump" or "stick" together after eating, when your digestive system is going through the digestive process. If they are still clumped after 6 hours of fasting, this points to the start of some kind of physical problem that warrants further investigation.

The clumping of red blood cells has been associated with at least 50 different kinds of pathological conditions. Red blood cell clumping or "blood sludge" may be due to altered blood pH, long term stress and toxic intake. High concentrations of undigested fats and lipoproteins have been associated with blood clumping. Not enough exercise, low minerals, metal toxicity, stress, allergies, low stomach HCL (low acidity) are also a few other reasons that red blood cells "stick" together. The pancreas may be off or it may simply be dehydration – not drinking enough water.

It is impossible for the battery in your cells (mitochondria) to deliver enough octane or ATP to make your body's engine work at optimum level when red blood cells are clumped. If the red blood cells do not have the appropriate nutrients to deliver, then you can be sure that the rest of the cells in your body do not have the proper amount of nutrients to function at your peak level. *An energy crisis develops.*

In my practice I look at blood all day long and analyze the shapes and patterns of red blood cells. You see a single drop of blood contains millions of red blood cells which are perpetually traveling through your body. I can tell almost instantly by looking at the red blood cells whether the body's energy system is off. If that is the case then I constantly ask myself why? What happened? What is going on that the red blood cells are not absorbing and carrying nutrients the way they should?

## I can tell almost instantly by looking at the red blood cells whether the body's energy system is off.

### Function of the Red Blood Cells:

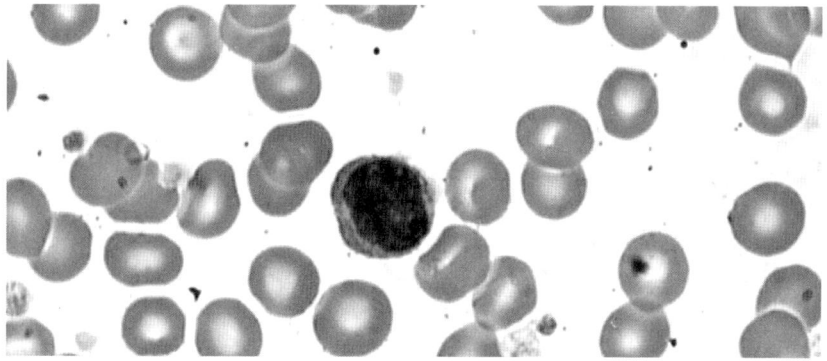

To get to the bottom line you have to understand the function of the red blood cells. Red blood cells contain a protein chemical called *hemoglobin*. Hemoglobin contains the element iron. Iron is what makes the red blood cell an excellent vehicle for transporting oxygen and disposing of carbon dioxide. As the blood passes through the lungs, oxygen molecules attach to the hemoglobin. As the blood passes through the body's tissues the hemoglobin releases oxygen to the cells. The empty hemoglobin molecules then bond with the tissue's carbon dioxide and other waste gases, transporting them away. Thus, red blood cells have 2 major functions:

1.  They transport through the body your oxygen, hormones, heat and all of your necessary nutrients needed for your vital organs and muscles to function.

2.  They act as a waste disposal company getting rid of carbon dioxide and cellular waste.

The body deteriorates at a faster pace when these two major functions do not occur at the level that they should. You talk about important little critters that are microscopic but so necessary.

Folks, do you know what anemia is? It's having a low red blood cell count. What is the result of having a low red blood cell count? *Fatigue!* That is why doctors will take tests to see if you are anemic when you complain of fatigue. Nevertheless, in my experience most people with low energy have enough red blood cells (so they are not anemic). However, they have red blood cells that are sticking together. This sticking together compromises the cell wall. This does not allow the red blood cell to carry enough oxygen or nutrients and therefore the body does not get rid of enough of the toxic waste (carbon dioxide and waste gases). It literally becomes a vicious circle.

What am I saying? The life of the flesh is in the blood. If you want to have life and have energy your red blood cells better be functioning properly. *Are you listening to your body's early warning system? Has your energy been low?* I tell you there is an energy crisis in this land of ours. No, its not the fact that the price of gasoline for your car is up, but people are walking around like zombies – *exhausted!*

## What Is Zapping Our Energy?

Over the years, what has caused such an energy crisis? *Why are people so tired?* Hey, I'm not talking about just being tired on Monday mornings after an exhausting weekend. I am talking about the energy crisis that has existed in the last 20 years. Before 1985 I never saw a single case of Chronic Fatigue Syndrome – there was no such thing. Since 1985 this condition at times called the

Yuppie Flu became an epidemic. In my thesis for my Ph.D., I studied Chronic Fatigue Syndrome and Fibromyalgia. I did extensive interviews with several hundred patients and found some common threads as we poured over their histories.

## Stress:

Stress can effect our bodies in several ways:

**Emotional** – This is a common stress that occurs to everyone at one time or another and our body is well able to deal with this in the short term. The Lord has given us adrenal glands "stress glands" just above your kidneys that are well able to handle normal every day stress. But, if that stress (a poor marriage, sickness in the family, financial pressures, a loss of a job, or working for a jerk at the office

**Stressed?**

etc.) goes on for a long period of time *we become susceptible to an adrenal crash or adrenal exhaustion.* This sets off a chain reaction in our body. Let me give you an illustration that might help you understand how the adrenal gland works. Remember, under normal circumstances this fight or flight mechanism is easily able to handle stress. Folks, a certain amount of stress is actually good for you. It takes the carbon build up out of the adrenal glands. (Not really carbon but you'll understand after I finish this illustration).

My wife's vehicle has a little button on the dash called turbo. When I drive her car (which is not very often), I like to use that button! When you push that button, does the car ever go (don't tell the police about it). One day I was reading my wife's car manual. I didn't understand a word until I got to the turbo button. You know what the manual said? "Turbo – only use to pass. Not to be used for normal driving conditions." Temporary use only – wow! Some turbo is good, when needing extra speed to pass, but too much for too long is bad for the engine. Prolonged use of turbo at one time makes the engine RPM's go too high and can literally damage the engine. Now do you get my point? Stress is actually good for you – your body can handle it. Too much stress over a prolonged period of time will damage your body.

**Environmental** – This is a new stress. People today like never before are affected by the environment. Let me give you some statistics. One third of children in North America today suffer from allergies or asthma. Isn't that incredible! When I started practice in the 70's that statistic was 1 out of 20. I mean when I was a kid (hey, it wasn't that long ago) I rarely saw anyone in my school with asthma. Now, today it is an epidemic. What's changed in the last 20-25 years that has made our environment so different? It's *chemicals!*

## Chemicals:

Do you know that since World War II there have been over 85,000 new chemicals created. Take out your cleaning products and anything you cannot pronounce is probably a new chemical that has been created. People today clean their homes and sterilize everything. They are so worried about germs but they never think about the fact that they are spraying hazardous chemicals into the air for everyone to breathe.

Most chemical products that you use to clean in your home would not be allowed on any industrial site without special warnings and special suits to handle them. Why? – because even minor exposure to the chemicals *can cause serious reactions*. Yet, parents think nothing of spraying the play pens, their kitchens and bathrooms with chemicals. People use laundry detergents like Tide that are full of chemicals. The residue left on the clothes are full of chemicals and that residue gets into the skin and inhaled through the lungs and literally stresses the body's immune system and adrenal glands. One popular children's brand that advertises their lotion helps soothe fussy babies at bedtime has a safety warning to keep out of reach of children, and to consult a doctor before using if the baby has allergies or asthma as serious breathing problems could occur. What is this poor baby inhaling? Even if this baby does not have allergies or asthma before use he or she most likely will after repeated use of this cream. The immune system is constantly under attack from a very early age.

## Since World War II there have been over 85,000 new chemicals created.

## Commercials:

Due to intellectual marketing campaigns people are buying into the need to clean their homes, brush their teeth, wash their hair, put on perfumes and underarm deodorant with thousands of chemicals a day. Our immune system is being bombarded from the minute we are born. The adrenal glands are in constant turbo mode. No wonder we see a huge increase in childhood cancers, Chronic Fatigue Syndrome and Fibromyalgia. *The environment is stressing us out!*

## Our immune system is being bombarded from the minute we are born.

## Tight House Syndrome:

When I was growing up in Northern Ontario, Canada, the winters could get pretty cold. I lived in Timmins, close to where Santa Claus resides. Better known as the home of Shania Twain. I remember our beautiful older home with lots of character. There were a lot of drafty areas in our home. When I would complain to my mom about being cold she would tell me to shut up (politely) and go put on a sweater. Today there are few drafty homes left. We have built our homes to be energy efficient. We have sealed them up so that air won't come in (hot or cold). That certainly makes us more comfortable but definitely no healthier. This has decreased our energy bills but has created all sorts of other problems by not allowing fresh air into our homes.

### The chemicals we use to clean are not even able to escape our homes.

## Wall to Wall Carpeting:

Another factor in environmental stress is that of carpeting. Once again carpeting is comfortable but it is a breeding ground for chemicals and dust mites that are microscopic. These chemicals and dust mites can create havoc on a person's immune system. When a patient comes into my office suffering from Chronic Fatigue Syndrome, Asthma, allergies or Fibromyalgia I ask them what their house is like? Then I ask them what their budget is like. They look at me like I have two heads. Then I explain to them the importance of cleaning up the home environment. I tell the patients that can afford it to remove all the carpeting from their homes and if that is not possible then certainly get them out of their bedrooms.

## Air Conditioning

You know I have air conditioning in my home, in my office, in my car. It seems to me that even though I live in Northern Ontario, Canada, where we only get summer for one month (just joking), I can't live without air conditioning. My sister has a car dealership in Northern Ontario and she tells me that they only sell 1 or 2 cars a year that doesn't have air conditioning. When I grew up there were fans but no air conditioning. Now air conditioning is great, except for one thing:

## Air conditioners spew out mold.

Mold (little mycotoxins) loves to set up house in your body. They have lots of offspring once they take up residence. They poop and compete for oxygen with your red blood cells. Literally, these microscopic critters can slowly seep the life out of your body.

## *Nutritional Stress*

## Sugar:

Nutrition is one area that has dramatically changed in the last 30 years. We are a people weaned on fast foods. When I started practice in the 70's North Americans consumed 30-40 pounds of sugar a year. Now it is a staggering 120-150 pounds a year. Can you imagine what stress this brings to our body? Do you know that the average soda has 8-10 teaspoons

•measure the cost•

of sugar? Sugar is hidden in almost every processed food. Just 100 grams of sugar (in any form) makes white blood cells sluggish within one hour of ingestion.

> "Sugar has increased from 15 pounds per person in 1815 to about 120-150 pounds per person at present. In other words the majority of people eat their weight in sugar each year. This comes out to more than a teaspoonful every hour, day and night." (Rudolf Ballentine, M.D., Diet and Nutrition – A Holistic Approach)

## Effects of Sugar on Your Body

☞ *Excessive sugar interferes with the transport of Vitamin C* by blocking absorption or increasing excretion of many minerals.

☞ *Sugar reduces the ability of white blood cells to destroy bacteria,* thereby reducing the body's natural immunity to infection.

☞ *Sugar increases the blood glucose level,* which leads to excess fat production. Excessive fat stores have been linked to colon and breast cancer.

☞ *Sugar neutralizes the action of essential fatty acids.*

☞ *Sugar decreases glucose tolerance* which strains the pancreas and potentially leads to hypoglycemia or diabetes.

☞ *Sugar increases blood pressure* which could eventually lead to stroke or heart problems.

## Sugar Wins The Triple Crown For Causing Bodily Harm

1.  It quickly boosts blood sugar levels.

2.  It increases insulin. This causes inflammation and accelerates aging.

3.  It creates a free radical factory.

"We need a maximum of 1 teaspoon or 5 grams of glucose every 3-4 hours to give our bodies and brains constant little spurts of sugar as fuel in our blood streams. We get this from eating fruits in moderation, vegetables, salads, herbs, sea vegetables (kelp) and green drinks. Eat just one average-sized commercial cinnamon bun and you get an overpowering spurt of 12 teaspoons of sugar, guaranteed to cause hormonal havoc by flooding and jamming your little engines into off." (Sam Graci, The Path to Phenomenal Health)

## How Things Have Changed

Read these two old advertisements taken from Ladies Home Journal – August, 1968 and Redbook, 1965.

# The name of the game is energy.

Billy never stops moving. Even when he's asleep, he's growing.

Kids need energyless, artificially sweetened foods and beverages like a china shop needs a bull.

Keep enough sugar in your youngster's life. For energy.

## Kids need what sugar's got

*. . . 18 calories per teaspoon—and it's all energy*

### Note to Mothers:

Exhaustion may be dangerous—especially to children who haven't learned to avoid it by pacing themselves. Exhaustion opens the door a little wider to the bugs and ailments that are always lying in wait. Sugar puts back energy fast—offsets exhaustion. Synthetic sweeteners put back nothing. Energy is the first requirement of life. Play safe with your young ones— make sure they get sugar every day.

# If your diet needs willpower, take a little sugar for your appestat.*

"Willpower I need.
Do I need an appestat?"

Yes, Virginia, you *do* have an appestat. Everyone does. It's like a "hunger switch" in your brain. When it's turned up, you're apt to overeat.

Sugar is quick energy. It turns down your appestat in a hurry. Even a little sugar can do it. Suddenly you may be less hungry and have the willpower to stick to your diet. And for a bonus, you get an energy boost, too.

Sugar helps diets work.
Why not yours?

Only 18 calories
per teaspoon—
and it's all energy.

I have been preaching against the high consumption of sugar for years. But, as you can see from these advertisements in the 60's the general public had no idea of the danger of over consumption of sugar. It seems to me that today there are still millions of people who don't get the message.

## My Wife's Story

We built our dream house in 1986 with an in ground pool, which she took care of, in the backyard. We decided to put a hot tub in our home. Wow, was that thing ever great!! No more going to bed with cold feet. We decided to put it near our bedroom. When the kids were settled in bed my wife and I would nestle up in that thing – well you get the picture. However, about a year later my wife who never had allergies or asthma developed both along with low energy and a multitude of other symptoms. Boy that wasn't like her – the mother of four children, a registered nurse, who was really a typical "super mom".

Rose-Marie was getting sicker by the day, until finally she was hospitalized. I'll never forget her doctor taking her blood gases and finding out that her oxygen level was really low. Anyways, to make a long story short, Rose-Marie was diagnosed with Chronic Fatigue Syndrome and Fibromyalgia. The doctor told her that this was a new illness and that they didn't know the cause and certainly didn't have a cure or even a treatment plan. My wife started improving in the hospital but as soon as she got home she would get really sick again. It wasn't long before we literally moved out of the house temporarily. Anyway, it took us a few weeks to figure out that it was the hot tub that was spewing out mold and chemicals into our carpets and walls. It cost us a fortune to renovate our house and to build a separate room for the hot tub with a ventilation system.

**It took us a few weeks to figure out that it was the hot tub that was spewing out mold and chemicals into our carpets and walls.**

# The Canary Story

My grandfather moved to Timmins, Ontario, Canada from Quebec, Canada in 1911. He was the founder of Martin Clinic in Timmins. Back then Timmins was a famous gold mining town. My grandfather used to tell the story of miners who brought canaries underground in the early days of gold mining. The reason that they brought canaries with them underground was to use them as an early warning system. In those days they had no measuring devices of odorless gases that develop underground and are quite deadly. When the miners saw that the canaries were dying they knew that they had to get up to the surface immediately. Well folks, today women and children especially are the modern day canaries. Due to stress in the environment, at home, or on the job women and children are taking the brunt of stress. They are the canaries that are falling first. *Nobody is paying attention!* That is why 90% of all Chronic Fatigue and Fibromyalgia patients are women. They are the canaries – much better looking of course. The world has changed. Stress is hitting us from every side. Guess what? Women and children are dropping like flies. Name every chronic disease and you will note that they affect women more than men. Children today are not healthier but are suffering from lifestyle and stress disorders like asthma, ADD, diabetes, obesity, autism etc.

# The Modern Day Woman – Super-Mom

There is much to be said for the advances that women have made in the last 100 years. However, from a medical point of view, women have paid an enormous price for their new found freedom. Women today compete with men in the workplace and are involved in every area of life with great gusto. However ladies, when you finish your job at the office, let's be honest, your day has only just begun. Women, when they get home have another job. They worry about their house, their children. They can't help it, they are built like that. Ladies, let me ask you a question? If your child gets sick, who worries more? You or your husband? You do of course. Why? – because men are from a different planet. It is not that we are insensitive – well maybe a little – but we are not programmed to worry like women. When the house is not clean – who worries about it more? Of course, ladies you do. Now what point am I trying to make? Well, competing in this world is tough enough. When you get home there is another tough job waiting for you. Listen, your body was not made to handle this continual bombardment of stress over a long period of time. That is why I am convinced that we are seeing an onslaught of chronic type disease occurring mostly in women.

**Your body was not made to handle this continual bombardment of stress over a long period of time.**

## My Mom and My Wife

My mom had eleven children. I get tired just thinking about it. But, my mom was not stressed like the modern day women of today. My mom did not have it easy, but she was not exposed to the demands of the modern day female of today.

My wife on the other hand had 4 children. They are all grown–up now with children of their own. Rose-Marie worked as a Registered Nurse, was involved in the home, kids, extra–curricular activities, church, career, exercised every day and lived in a modern home. This modern day home had all the conveniences such as wall to wall carpeting, air conditioning and a hot tub. She cleaned with every known chemical. Our house was always spot-less. You get the drift. You see my mom's life was a lot simpler but Rose-Marie's life was at a breathtaking pace all the time. Now add in chemicals, dust mites, mold and you have a recipe for disaster. That's exactly what happened to my wife in 1993. She was driving her body on turbo for too long and guess what? It crashed.

You want more proof that today's fast paced, stressed out world is taking a toll on women? When I started practice in the 70's 1 out of 20 women were diagnosed with breast cancer. Today it is 1 out of 8. You know it is getting worse every year. Men we are not much better off. In the 70's, 1 out of 20 men would be diagnosed with prostate cancer. Today, it is 1 out of 4 men after the age of 50.

Ladies, breast cancer is a lifestyle disorder. I remember in the 70's that we thought that breast cancer was genetic or heredi-tary. If your mother had breast cancer you are only 5% more likely to develop breast cancer. That's right, 95% of all breast cancer and prostate cancer are lifestyle related. They are modern day casualties of our hectic lifestyle.

"80% of women who are diagnosed with breast cancer have no risk factors whatsoever, except being a woman." (Dr. Susan Love on ABC News 20/20 – August 27, 1993)

## Other Causes of Low Energy

### Low Functioning Thyroid Gland:

The thyroid is located at the base of the throat. It has a right and left lobe. The right side is connected to the left side by a bridge of tissue called the Isthmus. The thyroid gland is stimulated by the pituitary gland to produce thyroid hormones (thyroxine – T4). This thyroid hormone (thyroxine) determines how quickly nutrients are converted into energy and also how efficiently food is burned within the body.

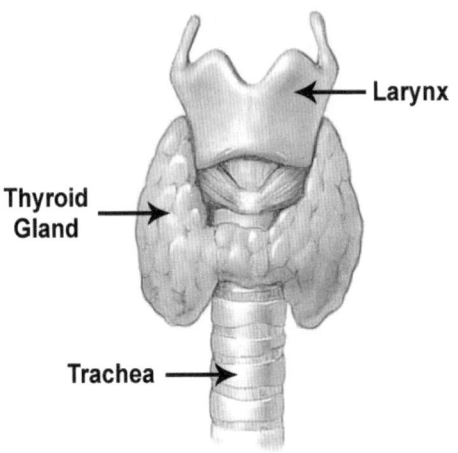

## Hypothyroidism:

Hypothyroidism, (underactive thyroid) happens when the thyroid gland does not produce enough thyroid hormones (thyroxine–T4).

## Symptoms of Hypothyroidism:

One of the first noticeable symptoms of a thyroid that is not functioning up to its optimum level is *inappropriate fatigue and weight gain.* Your daily routine is the same, you have not changed your diet and yet tiredness has become a part of your daily struggle. The weight starts to climb upward but your too tired to do anything about it. You go to bed earlier, but *restorative sleep evades you.* Even though it may be warm out, *you still feel cold.* Your moods, which up till now might have been fairly consistent, start to swing like a pendulum. Constipation, fragile hair and nails and an unexplainable craving for sweets, memory loss, irregular menstrual cycle, puffy hands and/or feet, muscle and/or joint pain, depression, sudden lack of concentration are some of the many symptoms of hypothyroidism.

## Treatment for Hypothyroidism:

Thyroid treatment is aimed at stimulating the body to produce *more normal levels of the thyroid hormone, thyroxine.* One of the ways that this is done is by restoring deficient iodine levels since the right amount of iodine is vital to a healthy thyroid gland. Treatment should also include the necessary nutrients that can help the body to function properly. The end results should be an increased metabolic rate and loss of unwanted pounds. Even more beneficial is the improved energy levels, a good night's sleep and no more mood swings. Once you start taking thyroid medication or supplements it will be every day for the rest of your life. It is like taking insulin for diabetes. Once your are a diabetic, always a diabetic. Once you are hypothyroid, always hypothyroid. The thyroid will need external support to help increase the level of the thyroid hormone. In order to help yourself when taking medication or a natural supplement you should get regular exercise, cut back on alcohol and smoking, reduce carbonated and caffeine intake and take at least 1000 mg of Vitamin C each day. If you are taking a thyroid medication, ask your doctor to switch your prescription to a medication called Thyroid. It produces less side effects. A natural product called ThyroSense is excellent for thyroid (Call 1-888-284-9920 to order this product).

## Hypoglycemia:

Several years ago you very rarely heard of hypoglycemia. Now it seems to be in epidemic proportions. What is it? What causes it? Hypoglycemia simply means low blood sugar. The average American ingests 120 pounds of sugar per year. The body cannot handle the concentrated sugars which often make up a large part of our diet. Low blood sugar has its most effect on the function of the brain.

Can you recognize yourself in this pattern of hypoglycemia?

➡ Excessive intake of refined carbohydrates.

➡ Rapid rise of blood sugar.

➡ Excessive production of insulin by the pancreas.

➡ Rapid decline in blood sugar because of excess insulin.

➡ Adrenal gland converts glycogen to sugar for emergency.

➡ Adrenal glands don't respond properly and don't know when to quit.

➡ Body needs sugar fast!

➡ Wrong food with a high sugar content ingested.

➡ Blood sugar rises rapidly and cycle starts all over again.

➡ Repetition of this viscous cycle occurs many times a day.

### Symptoms of Hypoglycemia:

Hypoglycemic episodes can minic almost every neurologic and psychiatric disorder. The most common symptoms of hypoglycemia include:

➡ fatigue, exhaustion, headaches

➡ irritability, insomnia, overactivity in children, behavioural problems, short temper

➡ eczema, hives, sinusitis

➡ nervousness, anxiety, depression, crying spells, fearfulness, personality changes

➡ inability to concentrate, forgetfulness, fog over the brain, prolonged sleepiness

➡ feelings of faintness, dizziness, tremors, cold sweats, water retention

➡ palpitations and irregular heartbeat

➡ inner trembling, shortness of breath, asthma, hay fever

➡ digestive disorders: colitis, diarrhea, stomach pain

➡ blurred vision, cold extremities

➡ craving for sweets, alcohol, coffee, or cola

➡ uncontrollable weight gain

➡ seizures, convulsions

## glycemic Diet:

The diet for hypoglycemia is as successful as you are faithful in following it. If you suspect that you are hypoglycemic, then follow the diet for a period of three weeks and see if there is not a noticeable improvement in your health and well-being.

➡ Eat several small meals a day and snack frequently on fruits and vegetables.

➡ Cut back on refined sugar

➡ Cut down on use of white flour

➡ Use low fat dairy products whenever possible

➡ Replace vegetable oil with olive, canola, or flax seed

➡ Do not grocery shop when you are hungry

➡ Chocolate bars are the worst thing to eat for a pick me up

➡ Cut down on or eliminate, if you can, coffee and alcohol

## Asthma:

One of the most prevalent conditions today is asthma. In my own practice approximately 1 out 20 patients that came to my office from 1974 to 1985 had asthma. Since 1985 approximately 1 out of 3 patients suffer from this dreaded disorder. Why such a drastic increase in this often debilatating disorder? Is there any help to lessen the severity of this disorder? I believe that asthma is *a classic free radical disorder* and one of the underlying factors in asthma is a condition called *hypoglycemia*. The body's cells have been damaged by poor nutrition, especially by the overuse of sugar and milk products.

The overabundance of chemicals in our foods – like food colouring and food preservatives – are also huge contributors to asthma, not to mention the often polluted air that we breath.

Research has now determined that babies treated with antibiotics before their first birthdays are twice as likely as antibiotic–free infants to develop asthma according to the March 2006 issue of the journal CHEST. Dr. Carlo Marra, an assistant professor in pharmaceutical sciences at the University of British Columbia in Vancouver said "people should not be prescribed antibiotics unless they are really nescessary." Antibiotics kill bacteria not viruses!

## Suggestion for the Treatment of Asthma:

Eliminate the following from your diet:

- ✘ Sugar
- ✘ Caffeine
- ✘ Processed foods
- ✘ White flour
- ✘ Alcohol
- ✘ Smoking

Cut down the following in your diet:

- ⬇ Fast foods
- ⬇ Fats (trans and saturated)

Add the following to your diet:

- ✚ Antioxidants (especially pine bark extract – take 200 mg daily for 4 to 6 weeks)
- ✚ Regular exercise
- ✚ Six small meals a day
- ✚ 8 to 10 glasses of water a day
- ✚ Positive mental attitude
- ✚ Increased fiber intake

## Fast Foods:

You know what the first words that came out of the mouths of my grandchildren? Not daddy, mommy, grandpa or grandma. It was McDonald's. They could say that name before they could say any other word. The problem with fast foods is that they are loaded with calories but have very little nutritional value. No wonder we see such a rise in obesity, ADD, asthma and other terrible disorders. *Our kids are overfed and undernourished.* A phenomena that I would have said would have been impossible is now coming to pass. I am now seeing my first cases of adult onset diabetes (Type II) in children. Most North American children are stressed out by their eating habits.

> "Under a mountain of fat, many obese people are starving to death because they are not getting what they need." (Rudolf Ballentine, M.D. – Diet and Nutrition, A Holistic Approach)

In Canada and the United states there has been a lot of concern about the future of health care. As a matter of fact to most North Americans this is the number 1 issue - not the war on terrorism, but health care. I am not a prophet or the son of a prophet but if something isn't done soon all the money in the world will not save our health care crisis. People think that to solve the problem all we have to do is just throw more money into hospitals and train more doctors. **Folks, unless we start by preventing disease, clean up our home environment, start exercising and eating properly, it won't happen.**

"More than three thousand food additives are used in the United States alone - dyes, artificial flavors, dough conditioners, texturing agents, anti-caking agents, and so on. The average person eats an alarming 14 pounds of additives a year." (Elizabeth Lipski, M.S., C.C.N. – Digestive Wellness)

## Sleep and Low Energy – A Nation of Zombies

We spend, or should spend at least 23 years of our time sleeping, if we live to the age of 75. Yet, *over half* the population in North America have severe sleep difficulties. Sleep disturbances is a consistent finding with patients who come to my clinic suffering from Chronic Fatigue Syndrome and Fibromyalgia. Imagine being tired all of the time and yet not able to get any type of recupperative sleep at night.

### Twenty-Five Years Ago:

Let's face it. Our world and our lifestyles have really changed in the last 25 years. I believe that some of these changes have contributed to our nation being a nation of zombies – exhausted all of the time. People just don't seem to be getting enough sleep. Over the last several decades, what has changed in our lifestyle patterns that has contributed to this "lack of sleep epidemic"?

### In the Past:

☞ We used to be more physical.

☞ We used to get more exposure to sunshine than we do today.

☞ We used to eat more natural foods and much less synthetic food or foods that have been tainted by antibiotics, herbicides, pesticides etc.

## Now:

☞ We sit for hours in front of the TV or our computers.

☞ We have much more exposure to chronic psychological factors, – social, family and at work.

☞ We have very little exposure to sunlight

☞ We experience very little silence. There is a constant bombarbment of noise from the radio, walkmans, TV, cell phones etc.

☞ We eat a lot of processed foods and generally have much more nutritional bad habits.

☞ We snack at night and too close to bedtime

## What To Do – Steps to Help You Get More Sleep:

☞ Exercise during the day but never within 2 hours of your bedtime.

☞ Meditation and prayer.

☞ Listen to relaxing music.

☞ Take a hot bath before going to bed.

☞ Deep breathing exercises.

☞ Increase your exposure to sunlight during the day which will help your brain increase melatonin levels.

☞ Limit your caffeine intake – remember a diet coke has 4x more caffeine than coffee.

☞ Severely limit your alcohol intake.

☞ Try natural sleep aids such as Kava Kava, Melatonin, 5 HTP, Valerian and Hops.

☞ Make sure that your clock has a red light and not green, since green light can disturb melatonin levels. Keep a red light in your flashlight instead of turning on the bathroom light if you should have to use the bathroom in the middle of the night.

☞ Never eat 1 to 2 hours before bed time.

## Immune System — Night Owl

Remember, when one sleeps, the immune system turns on in order to combat illness. The immune system including your white blood cells function much better while you are asleep. While you are getting your rest your immune system is working night shift. People who sleep poorly don't realize how much damage this does to the body's defence mechanism. Think of the last time that you had a cold – what do you feel like doing? *Sleeping!* That's right, your body, which is a marvelous machine designed by our Creator, works better when you go to sleep. The immune system does not like interference.

**People who sleep poorly don't realize how much damage this does to the body's defence mechanism.**

# Review of
# WARNING SYSTEM GAUGE #1
## *Energy*

1.  One of the most important keys to the delivery of energy is the red blood cell.

2.  Red blood cells transport nutrients and oxygen.

3.  Red blood cells remove toxicity from the body.

4.  Get a live blood cell analysis done.

5.  Stress – both internal and external will have a major impact on energy levels.

6.  Sugar really depletes energy.

7.  Immune system functions more efficiently when sleeping.

8.  If you have been tired for 2-3 weeks straight, your body is trying to warn you that something is wrong.

# Chapter 2

# WARNING SYSTEM GAUGE #2

*pH*

*For years now I have been* stressing the importance of regulating your body's pH (potential hydrogen). Your pH is another warning signal that the body is in trouble.

> "Every disease in the human body including high blood pressure, diabetes, cancer, schizophrenia and stress turns the body acidic." (Dr. Victor Marcial-Vega – Oncologist and Medical Researcher)

## What is pH?

The body is made mostly of water. Water makes up as much as 70% of the total body weight. This water is composed of oxygen, carbon, hydrogen and nitrogen. *Water is the perfect medium for the transport of nutrients and removal of waste products.* It is necessary for digestion of food, keeping tissues and joints moist, regulates body temperature through evaporation by way of the lungs and skin, serves as a medium for biochemical reactions, and maintains electrolyte balance of the body.

Water, just like in a swimming pool, can be measured. Water has either an acidic or alkaline pH. All of the body's processes are affected by the pH of water in the blood. The lower the pH number, the more acidic, the higher the pH, the greater the alkaline pH of the blood. The acid-base balance is charted on a scale from 0-14. The skin has a pH of 5. The pH of urine is slightly acidic at 5.5.

The pH of blood is 7.4. Saliva, which carries the enzyme amylase, the main enzyme needed to break down carbohydrates starting in the mouth, functions best in a pH of 7. Gastric juice in the stomach ranges from 1.6 to 1.8 – very acidic which is necessary for breaking down of food.

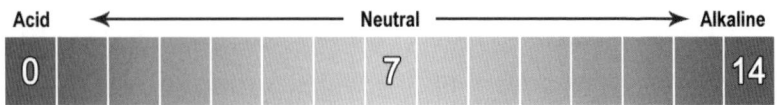

## Why Should I Be Concerned About My pH Levels?

Every function in our body has a pH that is geared for the work that is required for their specific function. When the pH of water shifts, the rest of the body is affected and chemical reactions cannot occur at the optimum level. *An unbalanced pH can be detrimental to our health.* Over the years of testing people's pH, I have noticed that most people that are stressed and tired have acidic pH.

## What Happens To Your Body In An Acidic Environment?

Think of the swimming pool. You look at the pool and you can see the bottom, it looks real clean and inviting to swim. You put a pH test strip in the water and you see that the pool is alkaline. However, the next day you look at the same swimming pool and it is very cloudy. You can't even see the bottom of the pool. Actually, if you took a few drops of that water and put it under a microscope you would see a lot of bugs, and parasites in just a drop of water.

Now, take another pH test strip and measure the pH of this water. Guess what? It has turned acidic. Folks, in an acidic environment anything can call it home – bugs, parasites etc. – *they love the acidity!* They grow and multiply in that environment.

## Cancer and pH

If you were to go down to your local hospital and measured every cancer patient's pH you would find their pH of their body fluid is highly acidic. Why? For their cancer to grow and multiply you need a highly acidic environment. Cancer cannot proliferate or do well in an alkaline environment. So friend, what kind of pH of your body fluids is important for good health? You guessed it! *Keeping the pH of your body fluids alkaline.*

**For their cancer to grow and multiply you need a highly acidic environment.**

## Another Example — Garbage

Have you ever seen what garbage looks like if you have left it out for a few days in the hot sun? You will see things growing and crawling in that garbage. Maggots and bugs will be having a picnic. Where did they come from? Well, when that garbage that is already acidic is exposed to heat and the hot sun there is a chemical reaction that takes place. This in turn makes the garbage even more acidic. You figured it out. This makes the garbage a major breeding ground for bugs.

# A Corpse

I feel sorry for police, coroners and search and rescue that find and have to work with decomposed bodies. What a horrible smell. There is nothing like that smell. Understand this about that decomposing body – the pH of the body fluids are very acidic. An acidic body that has no life in it, well you know it will have bugs eating it from the inside out. You have millions of little bacteria living within you now. Scary isn't it?! However, they are actually good for you. The minute someone dies these little microscopic bugs start growing because of the acidic pH. They start eating away at the dead body (I know that this is gross). But, this is what happens. I am using these illustrations so that you might more fully understand the importance of pH.

# Imbalanced pH and The Immune System

People ordinarily think of their immune system as a number of white and red blood cells flowing around your body. Most people know that white blood cells look for bacteria and viruses in your body and then destroy them. Well, all of that is true except the immune system is far more complicated than the red and white blood cells. The pH of a person's body fluids have an enormous effect on our body's ability to fight disease. We are not only talking about bacteria and viruses, but, also some of today's killers such as heart and cardiovascular disease, most cancers and a host of other problems. In an acidic environment your body's ability to fight any kind of disease is greatly diminished.

**The pH of a person's body fluids have an enormous effect on our body's ability to fight disease.**

## An Acidic pH

☞ **Increases the risk of cardiovascular disease and diabetes** – Acidity corrodes the body's blood vessels (we have over 60,000 miles of blood vessels) over a long period of time.

☞ **Increases the risk of cancer** – Once again cancer cannot grow in an alkaline environment but it will really proliferate in an acidic pH.

☞ **Makes the body age prematurely** – One of the most important factors in medicine today is anti-aging medicine. No wonder, every 7 seconds in North America someone turns 50. We might call them the golden years, but, generally aging is natural. Premature aging can really take away from having an abundant life. The balancing of pH is key to keeping your body from wearing out prematurely. Let's think about a car battery, remember it is acidic, if that acidity gets out of the battery you can see it on the battery terminals. What does that acidity do outside the battery? The answer is it causes corrosion. Acidity corrodes the body. Corrosion in the body will prematurely age the body.

☞ **Causes red blood cells to stick together** thus reducing oxygen and nutrient delivery.

## Batteries

Another illustration I use with my patients is that of a battery. Let me ask you a question? The pH of your battery in your car is what? Alkaline or acidic? Well, the answer is acidic. Why? An acidic battery is good for quick starts. Believe me you want an acidic battery in your car so that it will start quickly every time. Now let me ask you another question? The pH in your walkman and flashlight are what? You guessed it. Alkaline. Why? You want these batteries to last for a long time. You see when you start your car you need acidity for a quick high voltage start. After that your car doesn't run on batteries but on gasoline. If you want your batteries in your walkman and flashlight to last you need the eveready batteries with an alkaline pH. So OK. Do you get the point? Do you want your body to have an alkaline or acidic pH? You see the answer is alkaline. Why? Because you want your body to last for a long time. So think about people that prematurely age. They have an acidic pH. By the way. Have you ever seen someone that is dying of cancer? What do you see? A person that ages quickly before your eyes. I had a sister who died of stomach cancer when she was just 35 years old. Honestly, in the last few months, before she died, she literally looked like she was 85 years old. You know that cancer is rapid and out of control aging the body. What kind of pH is there in a cancerous body? Acidic! Man, you are getting smart!

## What Makes Your Body's pH Acidic?

### Stress

As we have discussed in the previous chapter, stress is a major culprit not only on your energy levels, free radicals, inflammation but also on pH. Remember, stress can come from three different ways:

☞ Stress from work, home, finances etc.

☞ Stress from the environment, herbicides, pesticides, mold, depleted ozone layer, chemicals in your cleaning products, dust mites, shampoo and deodorants to mention a few.

☞ Stress from foods.

## Stress From Foods

Most diets today cause an unhealthy acidic pH. Research demonstrates that when food is broken down and metabolized it leaves a certain chemical residue. Chemical residues when combined with our body fluids yields an alkaline or acidic pH. Here is a rule of thumb:

### All junk food measures a high acid pH after it is broken down. Every fruit and vegetable is an alkaline pH when it is broken down.

I know that some of you chemistry students are saying that this guy is crazy. An orange is acidic, an apple is acidic. But listen, after your body breaks any fruit or vegetable down they help to turn your body fluids alkaline.

## Weight Control

An imbalanced pH has a major influence on the body's fat storage. I have had hundreds of patients come to my office over the years and have said something like this to me. Doc, I hardly eat and I still gain weight just by looking at food. This I understand. Then I tell them the reason why this is happening. An habitually acidic pH can directly cause immediate weight gain. This triggers a condition called "insulin sensitivity" which causes erratic insulin production in the body. When the body is flooded from insulin it diligently converts every calorie into fat. Thus, an acidic pH will direct more insulin to be produced and subsequently demand the body store more fat than usual.

### An habitually acidic pH can directly cause immediate weight gain.

This is why people with Chronic Fatigue Syndrome and Fibromyalgia have trouble losing weight and steadily gain weight. They usually are storing lots of fat especially around the waist, stomach and hips (all the wrong places). This indicates acidic pH. So I remind them it is not how much they eat, but, what they eat. This becomes the real solution to their weight dilemma.

## Syndrome X

Jack Challem, a researcher and medical writer has coined a term called Syndrome X to describe a new condition that is plaguing North Americans. Syndrome X (Metabolic Syndrome) is resulting in a massive increase in diabetes, and obesity. *What is particularly scary is that Syndrome X is affecting millions of children.*

### What is Syndrome X?

Syndrome X (Metabolic Syndrome) is a nutritional disease. This condition occurs when your body's cells become insulin resistant. Insulin is a key to unlock your cells so that they will receive glucose (energy). When you eat, your body (pancreas) secretes insulin so that your body's cells will open up to receive glucose from your carbohydrates and protein. Now Syndrome X occurs when your body's cells become insulin resistant and will no longer open to allow glucose into the cells. Glucose that does not get into the cells for energy is stored as fat. That is why we are becoming such a fat nation. Syndrome X occurs when insulin resistance is combined with high levels of blood fats (cholesterol and triglycerides), too much body fat, and high blood pressure. There are millions of people running around suffering from Syndrome X.

### Glucose

Our body consists of at least *60 trillion cells.* There are not only red blood cells but also heart cells, muscle cells, brain cells, kidney cells and so forth. Each of these groups of cells have a speciality. Glucose is necessary to fuel theses cells no matter what their individual function is.

## What Causes Syndrome X?

Again, I believe that it is poor food choices. For example, today children are consuming 150 pounds of sugar a year. Can you imagine how much insulin they are secreting? They have cereal loaded with sugar in the morning or maybe a pop-tart. Snacks are full of sugar or corn syrup. Parents, *read the ingredients!* A pizza for lunch. Do you get the picture? A soda with 8-10 teaspoons of sugar washes down lunch. Calories are eaten with very little nutrient value and results in the pancreas secreting insulin all day long. Eventually, the cells of your body become insulin resistant. Syndrome X, by the way, is a precursor to diabetes. Honestly folks, I am now seeing cases of adult onset diabetes in children in my office – a frightening thing!

**Acidosis:** an acid pH is thought to be an important forerunner to diabetes. In the old days, before insulin was discovered, diabetes was treated by using alkaline powders.

## Quit Dieting

Diets don't work! They never have. They never will. I'll tell you why. Your body is smart. The second that you even mention diet your body says to itself – here we go again – and prepares the fat storage mechanism. Much like bears who hibernate in the winter. They store fat because their body knows that it is not going to eat for several months. Tell me that there is no God – who taught the bear to do that?

# Yo-Yo Dieting

Yo-Yo dieting is so common today. People go from one new guru to another. The South Beach, Atkins, Suzanne Sommers, the Hollywood Diet. You name it, I have seen it all over the years. However folks, unless your body fluids are alkaline, you won't lose a pound. If you do lose weight, it will be mostly water, some muscle and very little fat. If you can get your body fluids more alkaline you will lose weight and more importantly, you will lose body fat. Loss of body fat is more permanent compared to losing body water or muscle. When you lose only water guess what happens when you go off the diet. Right, you gain the weight back faster than you lost it and then some.

## Unless your body fluids are alkaline, you won't lose a pound.

# The Bowel and pH

One of the key organs in regulating the body's pH is the bowel. Yes people, if your bowel is not working well this will throw your body's pH off. Think of your bowel as the plumbing in your home. If your plumbing is broken, think of the problems that can cause in your home. The same thing in your body.

When you eat, your body starts the digestive process in your mouth. This is where carbohydrates start to be broken down by the enzyme amylase. Then it travels down the esophagus to the stomach where the acidic gases do a major breakdown. The small intestine is where your food is divided in two – what your body needs and what your body doesn't need. What the body needs is broken down into microscopic nutrients for your cells, then it is sent from the small intestine to your red blood cells for transport. What your body doesn't need is sent off to the large intestine and hopefully out the rectum.

## The Leaky Gut

Leaky Gut Syndrome is when the bowel or the large intestine develops small little leaks (they are microscopic) and can be caused by:

☞ The use of antibiotics in the last two years

☞ The use of steroids (cortisone or prednisone)

☞ Stress

☞ Long term use of NSAID's (non steroidal anti-inflammatory drugs)

☞ The birth control pill

☞ Chronic constipation or diarrhea

☞ Irritable Bowel Syndrome

☞ Chron's Disease

☞ Ulcerative Colitis

☞ Celiac Disease

The problem with leaky gut is when waste by-products, which should normally be expelled out of the body, come back into the blood stream through these microscopic leaks in the bowel. You have a major problem. This toxicity in the blood plasma will turn your blood's pH acidic and therefore create more problems in the body. Remember, in an acidic environment, bacteria, viruses and cancers can grow.

# Yeast Infections

I have had literally thousands of women patients over the years have come to me for a variety of health issues. A number of them come to get rid of chronic yeast infections. *The yeast busting diet does not work!* You cannot last very long on this diet because there is little you can eat. I give them a small lesson in physiology and how the bowel works. One of the most common unfriendly yeast organisms in our body is Candida Albicans. Normally it is kept in balance by friendly bacteria, but when the balance is upset, the Candida multiplies. Patients suffering from yeast infections that I have treated in our clinic have almost invariably been on antibiotics in the last several years or the birth control pill. These medications destroy the bowel's normal flora (lining of the bowel). This lining is made up of friendly bacteria. Now when that friendly bacteria flora is destroyed it causes a leaky gut. When Candida grows in number, the normally non-invasive yeast changes to a fungus-like microbe and releases toxins into the blood stream. This allows yeast, parasites and toxicity that ordinarily is excreted from the body to enter the blood stream. This, in turn, produces debilitating effects felt throughout the body.

## How Do I Know If I Have Candida (Yeast) Infection?

➡ Recurrent vaginal yeast infections.

➡ Recurrent urinary tract infections.

➡ Recurrent or stubborn fungal infections such as athlete's foot, or fungal infections of the cuticle or nail bed.

➡ Persistent bloating, discomfort and flatulence after eating; especially sweets.

➡ Chronic constipation or diarrhea.

➡ Symptoms worsening on damp days or in moldy places.

➡ Lightheaded and "tipsy" after a small amount of beer or wine.

➡ Severe fatigue and spacey feeling after meals.

➡ History of antibiotic therapy which preceded any of the above side effects which never fully resolved. (Dr. M. Rosenbaum and Dr. Murray Susser, Solving the Puzzle of Chronic Fatigue Syndrome).

## Treatment For Candida Infection

I suggest the use of probiotics (friendly bacteria). This should be taken for a minimum of 4-6 weeks. Yogurt will not do. You need to take a concentrated probiotic with a variety of strands of different bacteria. I also recommend the use of oil of oregano. This should be taken either as drops under the tongue or in capsule form. The best is in the form of oil of oregano spray. Try spraying your toothbrush (or a couple of drops) with oil of oregano, then put toothpaste on the brush. Vigorously brush teeth and gums. Do this for 4-6 weeks to completely eliminate infection.

## What Can I Do To Stop Leaky Gut?

Listen, sometimes you have no choice and have to take antibiotics. I don't like the birth control pill not only for what it does to the bowel, but also for what it does to the blood vessels by weakening them. This weakness in the blood vessels can make a woman more susceptible to having a stroke. Ladies, if you are on any of these medications, or have been on them in the past, then you need to reline your bowel with friendly bacteria. Now, you might be thinking friendly bacteria? Like in yogurt? Well, sort of.

Bacteria found in yogurt is acidophilus bacillus. This is only one strand of friendly bacteria. I suggest complex strands of bacteria. These complex friendly bacteria are like your internal army. They will reline your bowel, gut, esophagus, lungs, and sinuses to protect you from toxicity entering your bloodstream.

## 1) Friendly Bacteria (Probiotic)

In the next few years I predict that friendly bacteria will become a household name in natural medicine. In our day and age, with all of the new super-bugs coming from all over the world, and with the overuse of antibiotics, these super-bugs have become antibiotic resistant. We need a new treatment from this coming scourge. Well, probiotics are the answer. A major Montreal hospital was having real problems with a deadly bacterial infection called C-difficile. They did a study using probiotic therapy instead of antibiotics on this resilient bacterial strain. The results were astounding. Medicine is starting to finally realize that if we can build a patient's immune system to fight off these super bugs we are going to be much further ahead and maybe the pressure on the health care system can be eased a little.

Probiotics do much more than fight off these super-bugs. Taking probiotics will help you turn your body's pH more alkaline. Why? Probiotics stop the leak in the plumbing. There is no more waste that was meant to be excreted coming back into the blood stream.

## 2) Fiber

One of the key ways to turn your body's pH from acidic to alkaline is to increase your dietary fiber. North Americans just don't get enough fiber. Fiber helps rid the body of toxins by literally cleaning the bowel. Of course by increasing fiber intake you will decrease the bad cholesterol levels. It will also help you to lose weight.

Fiber is naturally found in plant foods such as fruits, vegetables, whole grains, beans and legumes. The recommended fiber intake, according to the American Diabetic Association, for a day is 20-40 grams. Most North Americans eat less than 10 grams of fiber a day. No wonder our society is so sick today. A simple thing like taking the recommended fiber a day will detoxify and keep your pH level within the normal range.

## Children and Fiber

Parents, you need to start your kids into a healthy eating lifestyle at an early age. Why? A child's pH is very important. Remember, cancer takes years and years to develop. Diabetes, asthma and obesity are mostly diseases that get their start in the childhood years. Parents, start thinking prevention at a very early age. Think, fiber, fiber, fiber for kids. Dr. Kranz Ph.D., who wrote in the February 2005 Journal of the American Diabetic Association says to change to "whole grain products and high fiber cereals." Children usually like sweet potatoes, baked beans, grapes, oranges, watermelon and they are all fiber. Not only that but they are high alkaline foods too! Parents, remember something, children are not stupid. They will buy into what you are doing especially when you start them at an early age. Talk to them straight about the importance of good nutrition. Explain what junk food does to them and their energy. More importantly, lead by example. I remember my 8 year old grandson telling me one day – Hey grandpa, that man over there is drinking a pop that is full of sugar – isn't he? I said "Ethan, you are absolutely right." He picked this up from his dad. Remember, kids are smart!

# Adults and Fiber

Adults should consume 20-40 grams of dietary fiber a day. Your mother and grandmother called this roughage. Increasing fiber intake is like taking a brush and scrubbing out the intestines where toxins have built up. Toxins are like indoor pollution. Over time this causes tiredness and an overall feeling of being unwell.

Fiber is an indigestible complex carbohydrate found in plants. It is present in fruits, vegetables, grains, and legumes. Fiber is not a single food or substance and it has no calories because the body cannot absorb it. Fiber is divided into 2 groups depending on their physical characteristics and effects on the body. There is soluble and insoluble fiber. Soluble fiber partially dissolves in water and insoluble does not dissolve in water. Each functions a little differently than the other and have different health benefits on the body.

Insoluble fiber is effective at increasing the feeling of fullness, stool size and bulk and helps reduce constipation and hemorrhoids. Insoluble fiber may reduce the risk of colon cancer and diverticulosis. Soluble fiber forms a gel-like substance in the intestine and increases the water content in the stool. Researchers have suggested that soluble fiber decreases blood cholesterol and results in lower blood sugar after meals for diabetics. They are both also low on the glycemic index. Insoluble fibers are a weight watchers dream since they contain fibers that bulk up and fill up space in the stomach. Therefore, we cannot eat as much.

## Soluble Fiber: (Acts like a gel)

➡ Fruits: apples, pears, blueberries, strawberries, prunes
➡ Legumes
➡ Dried peas

- Beans
- Lentils
- Oatmeal
- Oatbran
- Nuts and seeds

**Insoluble Fiber: (Adds bulk and softens stools)**
- Whole grains
- Whole wheat breads
- Barley
- Brown rice
- Bulgur
- Whole grain breakfast cereals
- Wheat bran
- Seeds
- Carrots
- Cucumbers
- Zucchini
- Celery
- Tomatoes

# Healthful Hints On Increasing Fiber In Your Diet

1. Choose fresh fruit rather than juice.

2. Eat the skin and membranes of fruits and vegetables that have been cleaned throughly.

3. Choose whole grain breads and cereals daily.

4.  An increase in fiber should also mean an increase in water.

5.  Eat less processed foods and more fresh ones or foods made from scratch.

## 3) Exercise and pH

Exercise, I have always said, is the great equalizer. Exercise is absolutely necessary in maintaining a proper pH. You know when you look at the thousands of studies done on medications and natural supplements you will get conflicting results. For example, look at the studies done over the years on vitamin E. Some results are positive and some are negative. However, when it comes to exercise, everyone is in agreement. There is only positive benefits that come from a daily exercise routine.

## How Does Exercise Affect The pH of The Body?

Whenever we work out, the body detoxifies and the pH becomes more alkaline. One important factor to remember is that when you are exercising it is virtually impossible to be stressed out at the same time. As you exercise your brain releases hormones such as dopamine and serotonin that calm you down. I believe strongly that the release of the hormones will help a person's pH move into an alkaline position.

*Remember, exercise does not have to be vigorous to be effective.* A study that I read recently showed that walking can be as effective or more so in burning calories as jogging or even fast paced walking. So the idea with exercise is to "just do it" as Nike would say.

"...researchers have discovered that a 30 minute walk can give a temporary lift from even major depression. Researchers at the University of Texas at Austin asked 40 men and women recently diagnosed with major depression to walk on a treadmill or rest quietly in a comfy chair. After a half hour, both groups had fewer negative feelings, such as anger, fatigue and tension, but only the exercisers said that they actually felt good. The walkers got an 85% boost in vigor (liveliness) and a 40% improvement in well-being. The lift lasted an hour. Past studies have shown that aerobic exercise increases the brain's levels of serotonin, a feel good chemical." (John Bartholomew, PhD., Professor of Kinesiology)

## Exercise Has To Be Consistent

Over the years of observing people I have found that consistency in exercise is the key. To get the real benefits of exercise one has to stay at it. Every January people make their New Years resolution that this is going to be the year that they are going to get into shape. However, by February or even earlier than that they quit. You know I think that people put too much pressure on themselves by having goals that are unrealistic. I am going to lose 50 pounds or I am going to train for a marathon. I believe that it is better to set realistic goals when it comes to exercising. For example, I am going to go for a walk or go for a bike ride every second day or 5 days a week. Then, as much as possible stick to it. You will be rewarded greatly. Believe me, along with good dietary changes your pH will be well balanced.

# Don't Overdo It!

The problem with exercise is that some people overdo it. When the Lord created the earth He rested after 6 days. Now He didn't need the rest, but we do. I strongly believe that by not resting enough, the body's pH, free radicals and inflammation start to cause real problems. Major league athletes that I have treated over the years have a problem in this area. With their grueling schedules, travel, living out of their suitcase, their body becomes exhausted. Whenever I work with teams I try and get coaches to give the team a complete day off at least once a week. When it comes to playoff time they will have more left in the tank than their competition.

For us amateurs we need rest one or two days a week. For Fibromyalgia or any chronic condition working out every second day is sufficient.

# Beneficial Reasons For Exercising

☞ Aids in fending off health problems such as heart difficulties, diabetes and improve quality of life.

☞ Exercise helps promote sleep.

☞ Coping with stress is made easier when exercising. Certain chemicals are released into the blood stream that makes it almost impossible to be stressed and working out at the same time.

☞ Exercise is great for your mental health and improving self-esteem.

☞ Assists the body in slowing down the aging process (how to age gracefully).

☞ Exercising is most beneficial for muscle strength and joint flexibility.

☞ Physical activity is a natural immune system booster and can give the edge needed when the body is fighting off an infection.

# How To Test For Your Body's pH

The most accurate test for pH is done by checking the pH of your saliva. A simple pH strip is needed. First thing in the morning, before eating and even before brushing your teeth, spit on the pH strip. You can also swab the inside of your mouth with a cue tip and then brush the pH strip with moist cue tip.

Don't use urine testing for pH as this is much less accurate. pH in the saliva should ideally be 7.0 to 7.4. This is perfect alkalinity. If your pH reading is below 6 then you are becoming too acidic.

☞ **If the pH is yellow (4.0 - 5.0), you are highly acidic.**
Start as soon as possible with a 2 day fruits and veggies only cleanse.

☞ **If your pH is below 6.0, you are too acidic.**
The body is starting to corrode. It is time to take this finding seriously and do something about it!

## Review of
# WARNING SYSTEM GAUGE #2
## *pH*

1. When you are acidic, you are sick! When you are alkaline you are healthy.

2. Increased acidity corrodes the body and causes pre-mature aging.

3. Increased acidity depletes the immune system.

4. Increased acidity combines with free radicals to cause an inflammatory response.

5. It is virtually impossible to lose weight if you are acidic.

6. Acidosis is an important forerunner to diabetes.

7. Having bowel problems such as constipation or leaky gut can cause an acidic pH.

8. Every fruit and vegetable once it hits your small intestine helps to turn your body's pH alkaline.

9. Exercise is important to keep one's body fluids alkaline.

# Chapter 3

# WARNING SYSTEM GAUGE #3

*Free Radicals*

*One of the first people to* talk about the importance of free radicals was Dr. Denham Herman in the 1950's. His theory was that free radical oxygen molecules acted like kamikaze pilots within the body's cells to destroy normal cells.

## What Will Keep You Alive, Will Also Kill You

Oxygen is something that we can't live without. However, the same oxygen that we rely on to live is going to guarantee that we age and die. The best example that I can give you is the apple. Cut it in two and within seconds

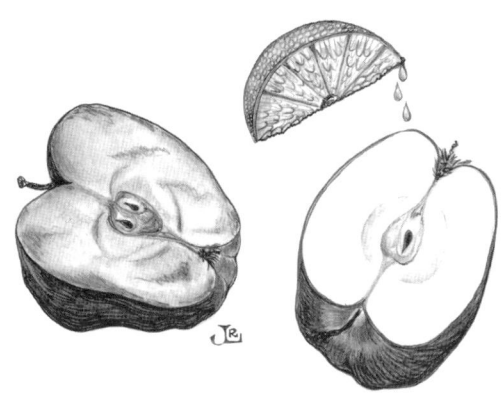

you will see what I call accelerated aging. Right before your eyes that apple starts to rust out. This mechanism called oxygenation is the same mechanism that makes us age prematurely. Free radicals can be an important part of our defense mechanism. On the other hand those same free radicals are the same mechanism that will end up killing us. However, if juice from a lemon (antioxidant) is sprinkled on the apple, the rusting out (brown) on the apple is delayed (anti-aging).

## The same oxygen that we rely on to live is going to guarantee that we age and die.

## Adam and Eve

When God told Adam and Eve not to eat the fruit of the tree in the garden of Eden, He wasn't kidding. He said on the day that you eat it you will surely die. Now folks, Adam and Eve should have listened. Since they disobeyed they have cursed the human race with a death wish. Have you ever noticed the statistics on death? One out of one dies, 100%. I believe that *because of the sin of disobedience God cursed the human being with free radicals.* You see Adam and Eve were built to live forever. They were never created to die. Their selfishness caused God to punish the human race with a built in mechanism that will eventually kill each and every one of us.

## Blood and Free Radicals

As I study patients' blood under the microscope I am amazed at how wonderful the Lord is. The Bible says that the life of the flesh is in the blood (Lev. 17:11). Now anybody that studies medicine and more particular histology (the study of blood) soon realizes that what the Bible says is absolutely true. Just try cutting yourself. If you don't stop the blood loss you will soon see the importance of blood. Remember, your blood contains all your oxygen and nutrients. Blood is an important part of your immune system. But, your blood is not perfect. Your body's cells last at the most for 1 year, then die. Thankfully, they are replaced. You acquire brand new red blood cells 3 times a year. White blood cells are replaced every week. Why do we constantly need to be replacing cells? God's curse has affected our cells and mostly the blood because the life of the flesh is in the blood. The wages of sin is death.

## How Are Free Radicals Created?

Free radicals actively takes place during the process of energy production in the cells of our bodies. The body also produces free radicals in the process of detoxifying itself. Free radicals, when in the proper balance, are used by the immune system to destroy bacteria and viruses. There are many diseases associated with free radicals. Cancer, coronary heart disease, stroke, arthritis, alzheimers, cataracts are a few to mention.

Through normal metabolism or exposure to pollutants, radiation and certain medications, oxygen molecules can lose an election and become unstable particles known as free radicals.

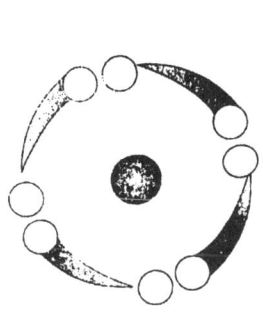

**Normal Oxygen Atom**

**Electron Loss Creates Free Radical**

# Free Radicals Set Off Chain Reactions

Seeking to restore balance, a free radical takes an electron from another molecule, creating a new free radical in the process. As each newly generated free radical looks for a replacement electron, a chain reaction is created.

# The Hazards of Oxidation

If this chain of free radicals is not broken, it can compromise the integrity of the cell membrane, ultimately damaging the cell.

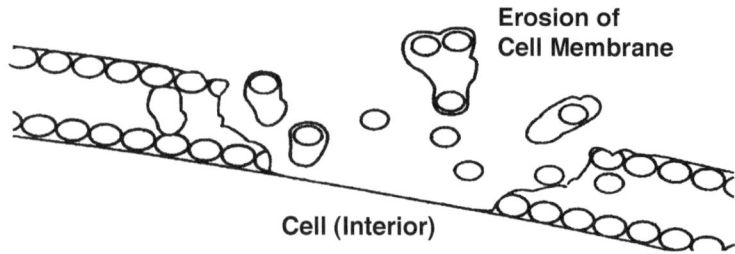

**Erosion of Cell Membrane**

**Cell (Interior)**

# *Antioxidants Neutralize Free Radicals*

The molecular structure of antioxidants allows them to give up electrons to free radicals without becoming unstable themselves. This effectively neutralizes the free radicals and breaks the chain of reactions.

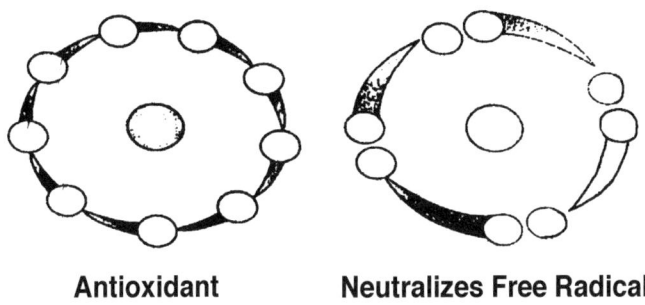

**Antioxidant**　　　　**Neutralizes Free Radical**

# *Cancer and Free Radicals —
Accelerated Aging*

Have you ever seen someone die of cancer? What happens right before your eyes is frightening. My sister Renée was a beautiful woman but when stomach cancer hit, she aged right before my eyes. A month or two before she died my 35 year old sister looked like she was 80 years old. Why? *A lot of cancers are caused by free radicals*. Oxygen molecules out of control. Free radicals react with the cells' DNA causing mistakes when the cell reproduces itself. If free radical damage is not repaired the DNA sequence will change. Scientists are concentrating on this area of research. If they can stop the DNA gene in the cell, from reproducing incorrectly then the cancer causing growth mechanism can be switched off.

This can be compared to a fireplace. A nice fire on a cold night warms the body. This fire is contained. A spark gets out and the fire cannot be contained. The house burns down. This is like the free radicals when they are out of control they destroy the healthy cells. Free radicals cause the cells to rapidly age and die within a few days. The body cannot replace the dying cells quick enough.

A friend of mine came to see me at my office one day. I had not seen him for several weeks. I was shocked when I saw him. He looked like he had aged 20-30 years in a couple of weeks. I asked him what was wrong, but, I already knew the answer. Sure enough he had terminal cancer. He was coming to the office to tell me about it. Look at a child that has leukemia and what do you see? Premature aging.

## Coronary Heart Disease and Free Radicals

Coronary heart disease or atherosclerosis, is one of the effects of rusting out of a body part caused by free radicals. This disease appears to be caused by damage to cholesterol carrying particles in the blood called LDL. The damaged particles are taken up by white blood cells called macrophages. These macrophages collect in the arterial wall forming plaque. The cholesterol filled cells attack other cells. This causes a growth on the inside of the artery which eventually slows and then blocks the flow of blood to the heart muscle resulting in a heart attack.

"Because cholesterol is found in significant amounts in the arterial plaque blocking the flow of blood, that cholesterol is responsible and therefore should be avoided. In fact, this is simply not true. If society were to use the same deductive reasoning, we would throw all policemen in jail, because just like the cholesterol they are always found at the scene of the crime. Ironically, both the policemen and cholesterol are at the crime scene for the same reason. They are there to save your life." (Robert R. Barefoot – Death by Diet)

# Stroke – Damage of Free Radicals On The Arteries

This is the same scenario as celebral stroke. Instead of the heart muscle, there is a sudden loss of brain function. This is caused by the interruption of blood flow to the brain or the rupture of blood vessels in the brain. The interruption of blood flow or the rupture of a blood vessels causes brain cells (neurons) in the affected area to die. The effects of the stroke depend upon where the brain was injured as well as how much damaged occurred. The bottom line is the effect of free radicals on the arteries.

# Arthritis – The Combination of Free Radicals And Inflammation

*Release of free radicals can activate white blood cells and cause damage to the cartilage in joints.* This causes a chain reaction of pain and swelling. Unfortunately, the statistics are now that most people over fifty have some form of arthritic problem. The belief is that this is cannot be avoided as the body ages. This is considered a chronic illness, one that can be managed by medication, but not cured. This is one of the most pervasive diseases and the leading cause of disability. There are many different kinds of arthritis, but the bottom line is the same – free radical damage. Scientists are now linking coronary heart disease and arthritis. A study reported in the December 2001 issue of "Arthritis and Rheumatism" suggested that patients with rheumatoid arthritis have a predisposition to atherosclerosis. They also have increased incidence of cardiovascular events compared with persons of the same age who do not have rheumatoid arthritis. This study was led by Dr. Inmaculada del Rincon, M.D. and colleagues from the University of Texas Health Science Center. Dr. del Rincon stated in an interview January 25th, 2002 that people with rheumatoid arthritis seem more likely than other people to have heart problems.

## The common thread between arthritis and coronary heart disease is inflammation and rampant free radical reproduction.

*Rheumatoid arthritis is an auto-immune disease.* The disease fighting immune system becomes confused and turns on itself, attacking tissue around the joints. Over time, a rheumatoid arthritis patient can be crippled by the damage done during this inflammatory process.

> "People with rheumatoid arthritis appear to have a double curse. Not only are they afflicted with a potentially crippling disease, they may be prone to early heart attacks as well." ("Arthritis double whammy" – article in the National Post, May 2005)

Now researchers suspect this misguided inflammatory response could also play a role in heart disease. The same overactive immune cells which are ravaging joints, appear to be wreaking havoc on blood vessels. This chronic inflammation might be setting the stage for an early heart attack.

Researchers at the Mayo Clinic in Minnesota recently reviewed the cases of arthritis patients who had been diagnosed with cardiovascular disease and compared them to non-arthritic patients. They found that arthritis patients had far more advanced cardiovascular disease at the time of diagnosis, compared to non-arthritic patients.

## Alzheimer's

This terrible affliction appears to have a free radical connection. Free radicals ravage the fragile brain blood vessels creating scar tissue. Early exposure to inflammatory disease multiplies Alzheimer's risk say researchers. The University of Southern California is the source of the new study on identical twins who suffer from dementia.

Margaret Gatz, lead author and professor at the University of California College of Letters, Arts and Sciences and her team which included researchers from the Karolinska Institute in Stockholm, Sweden, reached the conclusion that an inflammatory burden early in life, quadruples ones risk of developing Alzheimer's later in life.

Margaret Gatz focused her attention on inflammation because of the work of the University of Southern California gerontologists, Caleb Finch and Eileen Crimmins. They published a paper in the journal *Science* linking today's record life spans with the lower rates of infectious inflammatory childhood diseases – rheumatic fever and tuberculosis being an example of two of them. *Wow!* Inflammation seems to crop up everywhere as the root cause of many diseases.

# Cataracts and Free Radicals

A cataract is the clouding of the natural lens, the part of the eye responsible for focusing light and producing clear, sharp images. The lens of the eye is actually proteins suspended in water. Due to many conditions the precise alignment of proteins in the lens may break down and the proteins clump together forming clouds. This cataract clouding is actually a protein clustering. The lens is contained in a sealed bag or capsule. As old cells die they become trapped within the capsule. Over time, the cells accumulate causing the lens to cloud making images look blurred or fuzzy. For most people cataracts are the natural result of aging. Aging is caused by free radical damage. Cataract formation can be slowed by eating healthy foods. Eating green leafy vegetables and fruits high in Vitamin A, C, and E can retard the growth.

"There is a compelling body of scientific evidence that suggests that free radical pathology is associated with many of the chronic diseases, e.g., cancer, heart disease, and degenerative eye disorders, such as cataracts and macular degeneration. The evidence that the antioxidants may play an important role in promoting health and reducing the risk of several chronic diseases has been accumulating for over 30 years... everyone should be taking antioxidants!" (Dr. Jeffrey Blumberg; Professor of Nutrition, Chief of the Antioxidant Research Laboratory at the USDA Human Nutrition Research Center at Tufts University in Boston)

# Rusting Out — Antioxidants

Do you know the second law of thermodynamics? In a closed system everything deteriorates. For example, a cup of coffee if left on the counter will become lukewarm, then cold. I hate lukewarm or cold coffee. Even a new car will eventually rust out. People who are going to keep their cars for a while, most often will rust proof them in order to protect their investment and hopefully the rusting process will be delayed for a little time. Folks, that is how antioxidants work. They rust proof your cells.

**Antioxidants like vitamin E, beta carotene, lycopene, selenium, pine bark extract, grape seed and many others are antioxidants. They literally coat or rust proof your cell's wall from free radical damage.**

I remember asking my patients in the 70's to take Vitamin E and they would look at me like I had come from another planet. Patients are now much more informed. They know that antioxidants are absolutely essential for their well-being.

Your body has been cursed to what God has said three score and ten years. On physical strength, maybe another 10 years. Just in case you think God was not serious about this curse. Look around. The population is aging and generally we live a little longer due to the advances in modern medicine. Advances have particularly taken place in the areas of antibiotics and blood sugar regulation. But, lets be honest, with very few exceptions, once someone reaches the age of 80 they go downhill pretty quickly. Frankly, my goal is not to live to 120 years but rather to live as healthy as I can, for as long as I can, Lord willing. The study of human anatomy and physiology has definitely humbled me.

I am only 54 years old, but for several years now I have been fascinated by the brevity of life. The Bible says that life is short and full of trouble. It amazes me that man is so wonderfully made, yet, so fragile. I heard Billy Graham on Larry King Live say something that spoke to my heart. Larry King asked him after all these years what amazed him the most. Of all things that amazed him the most was the shortness or brevity of life. Here was Billy at 80 years old looking back and saying, man, it seemed like yesterday that I was 30 years old. Life is short and it seems that as you get older time seems to fly by even faster.

## Tests For Free Radicals

There are many ways to test for free radical activity in the body. These include "dry blood" or oxidative tests, serum and urine tests. The key role in these tests is essentially to determine whether there are sufficient antioxidants in the body to counteract excessive free radical activity.

Serum or blood tests are usually invasive procedures and may also be expensive. However, in my clinic I use both urine tests and "dry blood cell tests".

**An example of healthy dried blood.**

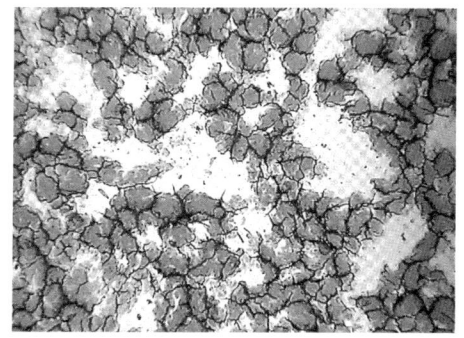

An example of unhealthy dried blood – excessive free radical activity has taken place.

Review of
# WARNING SYSTEM GAUGE #3
## Free Radicals

1.  Free radicals, if properly controlled, are essential to a healthy body.

2.  Excessive free radical activity has been associated with several diseases including cancer, cardiovascular disease, Alzheimer's and arthritis.

3.  Excessive free radicals cause accelerated aging.

4.  Some of the causes of free radicals include heavy metals, stress, smoking, excessive alcohol, air pollution, low intake of antioxidants found in fruits and vegetables.

# Chapter 4

# WARNING SYSTEM GAUGE #4

*Inflammation*

*Inflammation is another* Jekyll and Hyde phenomenon in our wonderfully made bodies. Without inflammation the body cannot heal from sickness and wounds. Inflammation brings extra blood supply to the site of injury. I call inflammation a sort of the Red Cross of injuries. You scrape your knee and right away the Red Cross is called. The Red Cross does not bring a band-aid for the outside wound, but, they are internal, bringing extra blood supply, nutrients, protein, fibrin and macrophages (white blood cells). This is called the inflammation response. People all over the world saw what happens when there is a poor response to a crisis like in New Orleans on the day after the hurricane Katrina hit. But, unlike FEMA, our body's response to an infection or injury is immediate.

The problem with inflammation is that it can become persistent and low grade. The medical world is just starting to understand that chronic persistent low grade inflammation in the body becomes one of the bad guys when it comes to your health.

Dr. James Joseph of Tufts University says that "inflammation is the evil twin of oxidation" (Newsweek, Summer 2005). In an earlier chapter, I explained the effects of oxidation on the body and how free radicals are important, but, also in some ways, deadly. Now what we are finding out is that whenever you find free radicals you also find inflammation. These two guys can be your own worse enemy.

## Inflammation and Heart Disease

We have traditionally thought that coronary heart disease as a cholesterol problem. The only thing is that 50% of the people who have coronary heart disease don't have high cholesterol levels. It reminds me of when I started treating people with Chronic Fatigue Syndrome in 1985. Some people were calling the illness "Epstein Barr Syndrome". However, only 50% of CFS patients tested positive for the Epstein Barr virus.

"Cholesterol reduction remained the Holy Grail of heart disease medicine until 2000, when elevated, silent inflammation levels, just below the perception of pain, were discovered to be the strongest, problematic component of heart disease, depression, cancer, arthritis, chronic pain, multiple sclerosis, dementia, Alzheimer's ADD, ADHD, and PMS." (Sam Graci – The Pathway to Phenomenal Health)

We used to have a simple view of heart disease. A gradual narrowing of the arteries caused by plaque build up in the artery (made of cholesterol). This could eventually lead to a blockage in the artery leading to a stroke or heart attack. Now we know that it is more complicated than that. We now know that when free radicals and inflammation get involved at a local level in the artery, that's when serious implications can occur. What scientists are researching for is a more accurate test to predict a heart attack or stroke. This test would be one that measures inflammation rather than cholesterol.

# C-Reactive Protein

A New England Journal of Medicine article in the year 2000 found that high levels of C-Reactive Protein – a marker of inflammation – increased the risk of heart disease by four and a half times. Another study published in the New England Journal of Medicine showed that post menopausal women with the highest CRP readings (C-Reactive Protein) were at four times the risk for artery disease than those with lower levels. A host of *other inflammation markers*, including interleukin 6, tumor necrosis factor-alpha, and adhesion molecules, have all been shown to predict future coronary events and stroke.

Friends, this is amazing because we have now found a blood test that can be taken that is relatively inexpensive *to give us an early warning of heart attack or stroke*.

Dr. Peter Lilby, Chief of Cardiovascular Medicine at Brigham and Women's Hospital in Boston said recently "inflammation is the alpha and omega of atherosclerosis." Study after study has shown that atherosclerosis, no matter what part of the body it is in, is related to inflammation.

# Obesity and Inflammation

The Center for Disease Control (CDC) in Atlanta Georgia said recently that about 300,000 U.S. deaths a year are associated with obesity. We know that fat cells produce inflammatory chemicals. Is it possible that these inflammatory chemicals make obese people more susceptible to asthma, diabetes, cardiovascular disease and cancer, when you gain weight, especially around the abdomen? These fat cells grow more biochemically active in turn, churning out more inflammatory compounds. As obesity increases inflammation, this inflammation in turn promotes insulin resistance, a central factor in diabetes or those suffering from Syndrome X (Metabolic Syndrome). Obesity doubles the risk of dying from premature death. The most serious threat to our future in health care in Canada and the USA is obesity. Obese children rate their quality of life as low as young cancer patients on chemotherapy. This was taken from a recent study highlighting the physical and emotional toll of being too fat. The Center for Disease Control said recently that there has been a 41% increase in diabetes in the USA since 1997. The link between diabetes and obesity have been well established. As a matter of fact, one of the conditions that I am seeing in my office that I thought would be an impossibility is that of *type 11 or adult onset diabetes occurring in children.*

Researchers are now convinced that one of obesity biggest side effects could be that of inflammation. I noticed this myself with my treatment of patients with Chronic Fatigue Syndrome (CFS) and Fibromyalgia. These patients were consuming less calories, but, in fact were actually gaining weight. Again, the inflammation response which is so prevalent in the patients with CFS and Fibromylagia caused them to gain weight and make weight loss an almost impossible task.

**Researchers are now convinced that one of the biggest side effects of obesity could be inflammation.**

## Abdominal Fat and Inflammation

A ground breaking global study by Canadian doctors show that routine cholesterol tests and BMI (Body Mass Index) are missing the true culprits in heart attacks. The study found in the prestigious journal "The Lancet" mentions that looking at the BMI is a poor prediction of heart attack. Instead a thick waist is a far more sensitive fore-teller of a heart attack says Dr. Salim Yusuf, a professor of medicine at McMaster University, Hamilton, Ontario. The study showed that having a fat belly was more dangerous than smoking.

Fat cells from the stomach ooze inflammation boosting proteins called cytokines. Cytokines dampen the body's ability to regulate insulin production and also paves the way for adult onset type 11 diabetes.

**The study showed that having a fat belly was more dangerous than smoking.**

## Diabetes And Inflammation

**Type 1 Diabetes:**
This is an auto-immune disease when insulin producing cells in the pancreas have been destroyed by the body's immune system.

**Type 2 Diabetes:**
This is also called adult onset diabetes. This has nothing to do with an out of control immune system response but rather years of poor health choices. Folks, anyone who has diabetes in the family should be very careful because then you become much more susceptible to getting Type 11 diabetes. However, if one takes care of themselves in terms of diet and exercise, Type 11 diabetes almost never will occur. In Type 1 diabetes insulin making cells are destroyed, thus there is not enough insulin produced. However, in Type 11 diabetes, insulin producing cells in the pancreas secrete too much. In this case the body's cells become what we call insulin resistant and the

cells will not open up to let insulin in. Your insulin is like a key that opens up the cell wall to allow glucose (energy) to get into the cell for energy. When a cell wall becomes insulin resistant the lock will not open and therefore all that glucose remains in the blood stream. Excessive glucose damages blood vessels. That is why people with diabetes are much more likely to have heart attacks, strokes, kidney disease, leg circulation problems, etc.

## What Are The Symptoms?

All types of diabetes produce similar symptoms. The most common symptom is fatigue, caused by energy deficiency and abnormal processing of fats, carbohydrates, and proteins. Insulin deficiency causes high blood sugar. High blood sugar, in turn, causes increased thirst, dry mucous membranes, and dry skin. Some people with diabetes may experience weight loss as fat and muscles are burned up to provide energy and excessive amounts of glucose are excreted in the urine.

## Long Term Effects

Long term effects may include retinal changes, kidney problems, atherosclerosis (plaque buildup in the arteries), and nervous system problems such as pain and numbness in the hands or feet. Other nervous system effects include night time diarrhea, and dizziness when rising too fast.

## How Is It Diagnosed?

The doctor will order blood tests to measure blood sugar levels. A blood sugar level equal to or above 200 milligrams per deciliter suggests diabetes. Another test for diabetes mellitus, called the fasting plasma glucose test, requires fasting for 12 to 14 hours before the blood is drawn. An eye examination may show retinal abnormalities. Other diagnostic tests include urinalysis and additional blood tests.

## Be Informed

Blood pressure, triglyceride levels and blood glucose are crucial, especially for women at risk for type 2 diabetes.

**Blood Pressure:**
Systolic – (top number) Optimal level is less than 140
Diastolic – (bottom number) Optimal level is less than 90

**Triglycerides:** Normal level should be less than 200

**Fasting Blood Glucose:** Desirable level is less than 110

**Cholesterol:** Total of 200 or below

**HDL:** 45 or below is good

**LDL:**
With few risk factors, below 160
With moderate risk factors, below 130
With heart disease, below 100

## Type 2 Diabetes Risk Factors

Type 2 (adult onset) diabetics have a two to four times increased risk of heart disease. When a heart attack strikes they are twice as likely to die within six months.

Type 2 diabetes is more common in women than men since angina – a common warning sign of serious heart disease may not be present. A woman may never have chest pain, she'll have jaw pain, arm pain, breathlessness or nausea. When women do get chest pain and seek medical help it is typically written off to stress, menopause or emotional issues.

The good news is that traditional heart disease drugs, such as aspirin and beta-blockers help to increase survival after a heart attack in some type 2 diabetes patients to a greater degree than in patients without diabetes.

## Fatigue and Inflammation

Anyone who is feeling tired all the time has got some inflammatory issues. As mentioned, in checking gauge #1, energy is a very important sign that your body is trying to tell you something is wrong. When you catch the common cold, get the flu or some kind of bug, you could almost sleep all day. Why is that? It is the inflammation response. Your body's immune system and inflammatory response is firing on all cylinders to kill the bug, virus and parasites. You are sore all over and exhausted. That's due to inflammation. So, do you see the connection in how low energy often times means inflammation? Remember, there is rarely inflammation without the evidence of free radicals.

## Cancer and Inflammation

Chronic inflammation also causes cells to oxidize which may trigger a cascade of cancerous mutations. Bruce Ames, a biochemist at the University of California at Berkeley, a former member of the National Cancer Institute believes "inflammation is responsible for up to 30% of all cancers" (Nov/Dec 2003, Journal of Alternative Medicine, page 67).

## *Chemicals and Inflammation*

Synthetics in our homes, glues, adhesives, pesticides, cleaning products cause more air pollution inside our homes than outside.

> "Cleaning products are of particular concern because we tend to think of them as good products. They clean our homes, kill bacteria and make everything smell fresh and flowery. But, everything that makes cleaning products good, also makes them pro inflammatory." (Dr. William Meggs, Ph.D., M.D. – The Inflammation Cure)

We are a squeaky clean society, from shampoos to under-arm deodorants to perfumes/colognes, air fresheners, odor killers, we are a society that can't stand odors or dirt. But, you know, I think we have gone too far. From mouthwash to douches, it's clean, clean, clean. We spray the play pen with Clorox or Lysol to kill bacteria for baby Joe. We use Febreeze on our sofas.

We spend 90% of our time indoors. So what we breathe inside our houses is going to really affect our health. Isn't it interesting that respiratory illness is the leading cause of admission of children to hospitals. Childhood asthma is up 400%. Dr. Gideon Koren a pediatrician at the hospital for Sick Children in Toronto asks, "how can we, as one of the most advanced countries in the world, allow these unsafe chemicals to enter our household for small children?" (Marketplace – Canadian Broadcasting Corporation television program)

# Top 10 Hazardous Household Chemicals

## Air Fresheners:

Most air fresheners interfere with your ability to smell by coating your nasal passages with an oil film, or by releasing a nerve deadening agent. Known toxic chemicals found in an air freshener: *Formaldehyde*: Highly toxic, known carcinogen. *Phenol*: When phenol touches your skin it can cause it to swell, burn, peel, and break out in hives; can cause cold sweats, convulsions, circulatory collapse, coma and even death.

## Ammonia:

It is a very volatile chemical, it is very damaging to your eyes, respiratory tract and skin.

## Bleach:

It is a strong corrosive. It will irritate or burn the skin, eyes and respiratory tract. It may cause pulmonary edema or vomiting and coma if ingested. *Warning*: Never mix bleach with ammonia as it may cause fumes that can be *deadly*.

## Carpet and Upholstery Shampoo:

Most formulas are designed to over power the stain itself, they accomplish the task but not without using highly toxic substances. Some include *Perchlorethylene*: a known carcinogen that causes liver, kidney and nervous system damage; *Ammonium Hydroxide*: corrosive, extremely irritable to eyes, skin and respiratory passages.

## Dishwasher Detergents:

Most products contain *chlorine* in a dry form that is highly concentrated. It is the number one cause of child poisonings, according to poison control centers.

## Drain Cleaner:

Most drain cleaners contain lye, hydrochloric acid or trichloroethane. *Lye*: caustic, burns skin and eyes, if ingested will damage esophagus and stomach; *Hydrochloric acid*: corrosive, eye and skin irritant, damages kidneys, liver and digestive tract; *Trichloroethane*: eye and skin irritant, nervous system depressant; damages liver and kidneys.

## Furniture Polish:

Furniture polishes contain *Petroleum Distillates*: highly flammable, can cause skin and lung cancer; *Phenol*: (see Air Fresheners); *Nitrobenzene*: easily absorbed through the skin, extremely toxic.

## Mold and Mildew Cleaners:

Chemicals contained are *Sodium Hypochlorite*: corrosive, irritates or burns skin and eyes, causes fluid in the lungs which can lead to coma or death; *Formaldehyde*: highly toxic, known carcinogen, irritant to eyes, nose, throat, and skin. May cause nausea, headaches, nosebleeds, dizziness, memory loss and shortness of breath.

## Oven Cleaner:

Oven cleaners contain *Sodium Hydroxide (Lye)*: caustic, strong irritant, burns to both skin and eyes, inhibits reflexes, will cause severe tissue damage if swallowed.

## Antibacterial Cleaners:

Antibaceterial cleaners may contain *Triclosan*: absorption through the skin can be tied to liver damage.

## Laundry Room Products:

May contain *Sodium* or *Calcium Hypocrite*: highly corrosive, irritates or burns skin, eyes or respiratory tract; *Linear Alkylate Sulfonate*: absorbed through the skin, known liver damaging agent; *Sodium Tripolyphosphate*: irritates skin and mucous membranes, causes vomiting. Easily absorbed through the skin from clothes.

## Toilet Bowl Cleaners:

Contain *Hydrochloric Acid*: highly corrosive, irritant to both skin and eyes, can damage kidneys and liver; *Hypochlorite Bleach*: corrosive, irritates or burns eyes, skin and respiratory tract. May cause pulmonary edema, vomiting or coma if ingested. Contact with other chemicals may cause chlorine fumes which may be *fatal*.

## Other Nasty Things That Are Around Your Home

## Pesticides:

Most pesticides have ingredients that affect the nervous system of insects. *Dimpylate* (better known as *Diazinon*): extremely toxic, impairs the central nervous system; *Chlorinate Hydrocarbons*: suspected carcinogen and mutantagen that accumulates in food and in fatty tissue – will attack the nervous system; *Organophosphates*: toxic and poisonous – if you can smell it, your lungs are absorbing it.

## Flea Powders:

*Carbaryl*: very toxic, causes skin, respiratory and cardiovascular system damage; *Chlordane*: accumulates in the food chain, may damage eyes, lungs, liver, kidney and skin; *Dichlorophene*: skin irritation, may damage liver, kidney, spleen and central nervous system.

## Lice Shampoo:

Especially vulnerable are children. *Lindane*: inhalation, ingestion, or absorption through the skin causes vomiting, diarrhea, convulsions and circulatory collapse. May cause liver damage, stillbirths, birth defects and cancer.

## Car Wash And Polish:

*Petroleum Distillates*: associated with skin and lung cancer, irritant to skin, eyes, nose and lungs. Entry into the lungs may cause fatal pulmonary edema, most are marked Danger, Harmful or Fatal.

## Tar and Bug Remover:

Contains *Xylene* and *Petroleum Distillates*.

## Warning terms used are significant:

**DANGER**– Harmful or fatal if swallowed. A taste to a teaspoonful taken by mouth could kill an average sized adult.

**WARNING**– Harmful if swallowed. A teaspoonful to an ounce taken by mouth could kill an average sized adult.

**CAUTION**– Harmful if swallowed. An ounce to over a pint taken by mouth could kill an average sized adult.

# What You Can Do

☞ Use environmentally friendly cleaning products in your home.

☞ Don't buy or use chlorine bleach.

☞ Use simple and inexpensive cleansers such as soap, vinegar, lemon juice, and borax.

☞ Avoid air fresheners and other perfumed products: Freshen your air by opening windows or using baking soda, cedar blocks, or dried flowers.

☞ Urge your schools and communities to use non-toxic cleaning products and to stop using pesticides.

**If the warning label says to use only in a well ventilated area – take it seriously!!**

You can use the following easy household recipes to help make your home toxic-free:

**All Purpose Cleaner:**
3 tsp. liquid soap, or 1/4 cup vinegar, or 1/4 cup lemon juice, or 1/4 cup Borax, per gallon of water.

**Oven Cleaner:**
Sprinkle salt on spills immediately. Use baking soda, vinegar, salt, or #000 steel wool. Clean grease with rag and vinegar. Sprinkle salt on spills. Let it sit for a few minutes, then scrape the spill and wash the area clean. For stubborn spots, use baking soda and steel wool.

## Window Cleaner:

1/2 cup of vinegar and 1 gallon warm water. Fill your own spray bottle.

## Stain Remover:

Soak fabrics in water mixed with borax, lemon juice, hydrogen peroxide, or white vinegar.

## Controlling Cockroaches and Ants:

Powdered Sugar and Borax. Combine in equal parts and sprinkle where they crawl.

# Testing For Personal Inflammation Status

You can test your inflammation status with your physician using the Silent Inflammation Profile (SIP) test that measures the ratio of Arachidonic Acid (AA) to EPA (another part of essential fatty acids found in fish oil) in the plasma phospholipids.

Nutrasource Diagnostics, associated with the University of Guelph in Ontario, Canada is the testing laboratory. Call 1-866-637-8378 in Canada or 1-800-404-8171 in the U.S.A.

A good SIP result is 3.0 and an ideal test is 1.5. *Reducing sugar consumption lowers excess insulin, which in turn lowers arachidonic acid, therefore lowering SIP.*

Review of
# WARNING SYSTEM GAUGE #4
## *Inflammation*

1. Almost without exception, whenever you have inflammation you will have fatigue.

2. Almost without exception, whenever you have inflammation you will have the presence of free radicals.

3. Almost without exception, when you have obesity, you will have inflammation.

4. Chemicals in your home create an inflammatory response in your body.

5. Having a simple blood test like C-Reactive Protein can determine years ahead of time if you are susceptible to heart disease or cancer.

**Common Blood Tests For Inflammation:**

☞ High sensitivity C-Reactive Protein

☞ Homocysteine

☞ Fibrinogen

☞ Serum Amyloid A (SAA)

☞ Pro-inflammatory enzymes
  – Cyclo-Oxygenase (COX-2)
  – Lipo-Oxygenase (LOX)

# Part 2

# THE SOLUTION

## 21 Days To Good Health

*In this section of my book* I will give you a plan to regenerate your body and ward off any disease that might have started. Am I saying that if you have been diagnosed with cancer or severe heart disease that you are now going to be cured? No, I am not saying that. Here is what I am saying. If you give your body the tools (especially your blood), then BY GEORGE! anything can happen. This is not rocket science. This is common sense based on 32 years of experience in helping sick people get well.

> "For years now, medicine has considered blood to be a sterile environment. But, they are wrong. Unfortunately, dead wrong for some of their patients." (Blood, The River of Life, Biomedx.com)

## Prevention, Prevention, Prevention

As I have often stated in the previous chapters, I would much rather help you prevent disease than actually have to treat disease. If after testing you have found that those four primary warning systems or gauges in your body are not right, then it is essential that you act quickly to start making the changes that I will recommend.

# Tests

What are the four warning systems in your body that will tell you years ahead of time that you are heading for disaster?

➡ Low Energy – get a live blood cell test.

➡ pH – a simple saliva test with pH paper.

➡ Free Radicals – a simple urine or live blood cell test.

➡ Inflammation – a blood test for C-Reactive Protein (CRP)

With this in mind, and your testing done, here is what you do to illicite marvellous health restoring changes in your body:

# Four Changes In Your Habits That Will Lead To Good Health

✔ Change #1: Change your attitude

✔ Change #2: Change your diet

✔ Change #3: Change your exercise

✔ Change #4: Change your supplements

# Chapter 5

# CHANGE #1

## Change Your Attitude

*Some say that attitude is* everything when it comes to wellness. Well, it is not everything, but it sure is important. I want to start this section with attitude because having a good attitude is foundational to helping your body help itself.

"For as he thinks in his heart, so is he." (Proverbs 23:7 – Holy Bible, New King James Version)

## My Dad's Story

My father passed away on July 5th, 2005 after a courageous battle with cancer. He was 80 years old. My dad was a real hero to me and I miss him dearly. Whenever I get a chance to talk to people about God's goodness and plan of salvation I let them know that I had no trouble believing in a loving God because of the father I had. My father was consistent in his love – well I could go on and on. However, it is how my dad dealt with the diagnosis of diabetes when he was forty years old that I will share with you.

When I was about sixteen years old, my dad came home one day and told me that he was a diabetic. Well, when I was sixteen, I had no idea what diabetes was all about. I knew that my grandfather had died from diabetes. My dad had not been feeling the greatest for a while, but having the diagnosis of diabetes kind of left an impression on me.

I remember the next day like it were yesterday. When I got

127

up to go to school the next morning, I saw my dad running on the spot in our family living room. "Dad, what are you doing?" I asked. I remember that he used the word "jogging" and I am sure that was the first time I ever heard that word. Then I asked another question. "Dad, why are you jogging?" His answer I can still hear today. "Son, our family doctor told me yesterday that I was a diabetic and that *if I didn't change my lifestyle I would be dead in five years or less.*" Wow, did that ever have an impact on me. Well, it didn't take long for the changes that my father implemented in his life to have a huge impact on my father's health. My father was always a big man and somewhat obese. Within two to three months he lost forty pounds and jogged every day (now he started running outside because my mom was ready to kill him for wearing out the carpet). Some of the biggest changes occurred in my dad's dietary habits. He cut out desserts and would add sugar to absolutely nothing. I recall my dad drinking a soft drink called "Tab". I believe that it was the first sugar free diet soda that one could drink. Man, did that stuff ever taste bad. My dad was a real trooper, he was disciplined. I decided to join my dad. I loved his company so much that I got up early in the morning to go jogging with him. You know what? I lost twenty-five pounds way back then and I've tried to stay in great shape ever since.

## Tale of Two Men

On the same day that my dad announced to us that he was a diabetic, a good friend of his was also diagnosed as a diabetic. But, here is the difference. My friend's father made absolutely no changes in his lifestyle. He even doubted that he was a diabetic – "never liked doctors" he used to say. You know, my friend's dad died four years after the diagnosis. Yes, in 1972 my friends died of the complications of diabetes. Why do I tell you this story? *Having the right attitude is the key to your health.*

You see, my dad had the right attitude. Folks, information provides power to choose. My father had made the right choices. He had a great attitude, and my friend's dad had a poor attitude and it cost him big time.

## 21 Days Towards Good Health

Over the years of observing human behaviour I have developed a strategy to help people achieve their goals when it comes to their health. I see myself as more of a coach, knowing that I am not able to go home with my patients to implement health changes. However, I can most help by giving them a plan to achieve good health. I first talk to my patients about setting realistic goals and giving them a little lesson in human psychology.

People need to understand that new habits are formed in just twenty-one days. That's right, people can see a good habit formed in just three weeks. I use two examples in my own life that will illustrate this point.

## My Love of Soft Drinks

When I first started practice in 1974 I used to keep soft drinks in my personal fridge at the office and sip on these drinks. Several times a day I would go to the fridge and easily go through three to four cans of soda a day. I knew that it wasn't good for me, but, hey I liked it! Then I remember one day saying to myself, "Tony, you know drinking this stuff is not good for you. You need to stop." So I went cold turkey and it was tough for the first couple of weeks. Of course I substituted the colas with water (you always need a substitute). Well, within three weeks I had lost my love for sodas. As a matter of fact, I rarely drink a soda today. You see it was tough for the first couple of weeks, but then your body changes and you can form a new, healthier habit.

## Coffee With Sugar

I love coffee and I try to limit myself to one or two cups of coffee a day. However, when I first started drinking coffee I used to drink it with at least four teaspoons of sugar. Once again, there came a time knowing that all that sugar was not good for me. I knew I had to change this habit. It was tough for a few weeks as I weaned myself off sugar in my coffee. But amazingly, after three weeks I really lost my sweet tooth when it came to adding sugar in my coffee. You know it has gotten so bad that if someone has added even a grain of sugar in my coffee by mistake, I won't drink it. That sweet taste has become repulsive to me.

## Works For Everybody

When I send my patients home with a plan to start exercising or cutting out a certain foods, or even adding a health altering food to their diet, I always explain the twenty-one day rule. I strongly urge them to commit to introducing this change and not give up. I had a lady in my office last month who was suffering from severe headaches. When looking at her blood I was able to determine that she was suffering from dehydration. This lady had trouble accepting the fact that she had to drink more water. I can still hear her arguments. "I am not thirsty, I don't like water." I promised her that if she would commit to drinking three to four glasses of water a day (or more if she could), in three weeks she would take a liking to water. She would also realize how thirsty she really was and thirdly, her headaches would go away. Guess what? She called me last week to thank me and said that her headaches were gone. She couldn't believe that she now actually liked water. It's only a matter of changing your habits.

## 42 Days

Yes, it only takes twenty-one days to change a habit, but *to reinforce that change and make the change permanent will require six weeks or fourty-two days.*

## The Three D's

Another little pep talk that I have with my patients concerns the three D's. The three D's represent:

☞ Desire
☞ Determination
☞ Discipline

Once again, my observing of human behaviour in my patients in the last thirty-two years has been quite helpful. I have determinded that in order for a person to fully achieve their health goals from losing weight to making a comeback after a long illness they need to understand the three D's. Let me explain.

## Desire – The Mind

A lot of people want to be healthy. A lot of people want to lose weight. They have a desire. I have not met many smokers that do not want to quit smoking. I have not yet met anyone that is carrying a little extra weight that doesn't want to lose those extra pounds. I have rarely met an alcoholic that doesn't regret every time that they drink. They have a desire to stop. But, just having a desire will not do it. Of course it is a step, but it is just the first step in implementing any change.

## Determination – The Heart

The second step in implementing any change is determination. Now when a person makes a committment and they are determined to accomplish their goals, it goes from the head to the heart. This eighteen inches is crucial. The desire is now taking seed and determination is now making that seed grow.

## Discipline – The Body

Discipline is the third positive attitude change that needs to take place in order for one to achieve their health goals. Whereas desire involves a change in thinking (mind), determination involves a change in heart. Discipline is the day-to-day, in the trenches attitude that will get you through these implemented changes and the tough times associated with these changes. Folks, if you are going to make changes you know that it is not going to be smooth sailing. Discipline involves sticking to it in the difficult times. I have found that the personal friends that we have think that they are all doctors. What do I mean? Well, people are real good at handing out advice on subjects (especially health) that they know very little about. You don't know how many times that I have sent a patient home with a plan to get well, that included dietary changes, supplement changes and they call me back in one week and say "My friend told me that I should try this other thing or try that thing." I say to them "No". Stick to the plan that I gave you. Don't deviate from it and it will work – but you must stick to it. Discipline involves going around the day-to-day land mines that are there to stop you from reaching your goals.

## Watch Out For The Land Mines

➡ Know-it-all friends.

➡ People who think they have the gift of discouragement.

➡ Stress

## Rewards

Another area of human behaviour that I discuss with my patients is that of the reward system. Rewards provide ample motivation for one to stick to the goals and make permanent lifestyle changes. I suggest to my patients that they eliminate the word "never" from their vocabulary. Examples of this are: "I will never have another piece of chocolate cake," "I will stop eating chocolates," "I will never have ice cream again."

I suggest to all of my patients to implement the reward system into their health goals. For example, why not have dessert once or twice a week if you have been making good and healthy changes to your lifestyle. I find that by adding a reward system people have an easier time sticking to these healthy changes forever. In my own case, like I said before, I love my coffee. Rather than eliminate coffee, I use it as a reward for good behaviour. In the morning, after I go for my run (over 38 years of sticking to it), I look forward to my "reward" of having a coffee. You see this reward stimulates me and encourages me to stick to it.

## Rewards Work!

# Chapter 6

# CHANGE #2

# Change Your Diet

## "We are digging our grave with our teeth."
**–Author Unknown**

*In this section I want to* talk about the most important part of this whole book. What I am going to share with you about food choices will become critical in your quest for optimum health. The food choices that you make every meal are essential to your body in terms of energy, making one more alkaline, reducing free radicals and inflammation.

> "It's not drugs and alcohol that are the drugs of choice these days – it's food" (J. Bains, Neuroscientist and Associate Professor – University of Calgary)

## No Neutral Foods

Friends, if you learn nothing else from this book please remember this: *What you put in your mouth every day will either be a positive or negative experience*, due to our high stressed and fast paced lifestyles. Then add in soil erosion, the use of pesticides, herbicides and hormones in our plant foods and meats. Folks, there are no neutral foods. Yes, everything you put into your mouth, including what you drink, will be a benefit or be detrimental to your health.

"The old saying 'You are what you eat' is primarily true. From birth to death, we continually create and re-create ourselves from the nourishment we put inside the body." (Elizabeth Lipski, M.S., C.C.N., Digestive Wellness)

I am going to make a couple of blanket statements concerning all fruits and all vegetables. *Every fruit and vegetable that you eat will help in the following areas:*

☞ Turn your body fluid from acidic to alkaline. Every fruit and every vegetable, even though some like oranges that are acidic pH, once they hit your small intestine, they change to alkaline.

☞ The high fiber content of fruits and veggies help to:
a) control blood sugar.
b) scrub the bowel and thus eliminate toxins, which will make you more alkaline and reduce free radical activity.

☞ The antioxidant content of fruits and veggies help reduce free radicals.

☞ According to a recent study, most people do not eat enough fruits and vegetables. Many associations, including the Canadian and American Cancer Society have urged consumers to eat between 5-10 daily servings of fruits and veggies. The American Journal of Public Health reported recently that there has been a negligible increase in fruit and vegetable consumption. In 1990 only 19% of Americans ate 5 servings of fruit and vegetables. In the year 2000, it was only up to 23%.

# Start Your Day With Dr Martin's Perfect Smoothie

This smoothie was designed for the ultimate protection against free radicals and provides a turbo boost for your energy level. This delicious smoothie will help turn your body fluids alkaline and will reduce inflammation in your body.

## Preparation:

1.  Mix a combination of fresh or frozen fruit such as: raspberries, blueberries (preferably wild) and strawberries etc.
    a) apple with skin
    b) half a banana

2.  Orange juice – (enough for one glass) not from concentrate and the more pulp the better

3.  Hemp Seed Protein Powder, 1 scoop

4.  Flax Seeds – 2 tablespoons

Use a blender or juicer. I use a Vita-Mix Machine.

"We have only scratched the surface in understanding the nutritional value of God's plant food." (Dr. Patrick Quillin – Healing Secrets from the Bible)

# Plant Foods

Did you know that plant foods contain:

☞ Over 20,000 different bioflavonoids in plant foods are known to be great free radical scavengers and these bioflavonoids help to chelate toxic metals out of our bodies.

☞ Over 800 different carotenoids to stimulate the immune system function.

☞ Abundant potassium for regulating cell function.

☞ An endless list of health-giving substances.

## Dr Martin's 10 Favorite Foods For Maximum Health Benefits

### Apples

An apple a day keeps the doctor away. Apples contain several phytonutrients including:

➡ Pectin – a soluble fiber helps lower blood cholesterol.

➡ Calcium pyruvate – which helps to regulate blood sugar.

Other benefits of apples:

➡ Apples have long been called nature's tooth brush. Biting on an apple stimulates the gums and promotes dental hygiene.

➡ Helps prevent bad breath.

➡ Helps you to become more alkaline.

➡ Low on the glycemic index – meaning the secretion of insulin is minimal.

### Grapefruit

➡ A good source of folate, iron, calcium and other minerals.

➡ High in beta carotene a precursor to vitamin A.

➡ High in fiber and low in calories.

➡ Low on the glycemic index.

➡ High in lycopene – great for men with prostate problems.

"Guess what one thing is not being washed and cleansed on a regular basis in this country? The inside of our bodies! The only way this can be done is by eating foods that are high in water content. Drinking water won't do it because drinking water does not carry the enzymes and other life preserving elements into the body that the water in fruits and vegetables does." (Harvey and Marilyn Diamond – Fit for Life)

## Red Grapes

➡ Green grapes are good, but, red grapes are better.

➡ High in pectin and bioflavonoids.

➡ Low calorie snack

➡ Low on the glycemic index

➡ Contains quercitin, a natural anti-inflammatory.

➡ Lowers blood cholesterol.

➡ Reduces the action of platelets making them less sticky, therefore reducing the risk of strokes and blood clots.

## Whole Grains

➡ Rich in complex carbohydrates which simply means they break down slowly in your blood stream. This makes them excellent for blood sugar issues and healthy weight loss.

➡ Rich in fiber to scrub the bowel.

➡ Lowers bad cholesterol.

➡ Very low in fat.

➡ A good source of protein.

➡ One drawback to be careful of is gluten allergies (celiac disease).

## Good Grains

Barley, millet, oat bran, oats, rolled oats, brown rice, whole wheat, rye, and malt. Barley is rich in tocotricnols, which helps to reduce free radicals (more potent than Vitamin E). There is also less risk of an allergic reaction with barley.

## Bananas

➡ A good source of potassium, folate and Vitamin C and B6.

➡ A banana a day is essential for people with Fibromyalgia because they are an excellent source of potassium which helps damaged muscles.

➡ A banana also contains prebiotics which help feed your friendly bacteria in the gut.

➡ An excellent source of fiber.

**Slight Drawback:** A little high on the glycemic index but, it has so many advantages that I highly recommend them.

## Oranges

➡ An excellent source of Vitamin C.

➡ A good source of beta carotene, potassium, folate, and thiamine.

➡ Contains pectin – a dietary fiber that helps lower cholesterol.

➡ Freshly squeezed oranges are the best form, try to stay away from "made from concentrate."

## Blueberries, Raspberries, Strawberries

➡ A great source of anthocyadins – a powerful antioxidant due to its good bioflavonoid content.

➡ Reduces urinary tract infections.

➡ Great source of fibers and pectin.

## Celery

➡ Great source of fiber, water and very low in calories.

➡ Good source of potassium.

➡ Reduces inflammation due to the amount of polyacetylene, that reduces prostaglandins (body chemicals that are instrumental in producing inflammation).

## Deeply Colored Peppers

➡ High in bioflavonoids which help to prevent cancer by reducing free radicals.

➡ Contains phenolic acid – inhibits the formation of cancer causing nitrosamines.

➡ Contains plant sterols that lower cholesterol.

➡ Contains more Vitamin C than citrus fruits.

## Broccoli and Brussel Sprouts

➡ One of the most nutritious vegetables. Over the last 20 years there have been several studies to show that they reduce the risk of cancer of the colon, breast, cervix, lungs, prostate, esophagus, larynx and bladder.

➡ High in indoles – a plant chemical that reduces the risk of cancer.

➡ Rich in bioflavonoids.

➡ A great source of protein, calcium, iron and trace minerals.

➡ An excellent source of Vitamin C.

## Dr Martin's Food Rating: The Good, The Bad, The Ugly

## The Good

✓ Every fruit and every vegetable.

✓ Fish – especially fatty fish like herring, mackerel, salmon, trout, and pickerel.

✓ Eggs

✓ Beans

✓ Barley, whole grain, millet.

✓ Chicken (not breaded), low fat beef, turkey, liver.

✓ Pumkin seeds, sunflower seeds, sesame seeds, hemp seeds, flax seeds.

✓ Nuts (watch for allergies)

✓ Green tea

✓ Coffee (one a day), not decaffinated.

✓ Soy milk

✓ Homemade peanut butter with no sugar or preservatives added.

✓ Honey and maple syrup (in small amounts).

✓ Low fat cheese

✓ Juices that are not "made from concentrate".

✓ Oil & vinegar dressing – use extra virgin olive oil (cold pressed).

"People of America, the greatest threat to the survival of you and your children is not some terrible nuclear weapon. It is what you are going to eat from your dinner plate tonight." (Dr. David Reuben, Everything You Always Wanted To Know About Nutrition)

## The Bad

✗ Fruit juices from concentrate.

✗ Milk, ice cream.

✗ White rice and white bread.

✗ Pancakes and waffles.

✗ Canned fruit especially with sugar added.

✗ Pork and pork sausages.

✗ Bologna, hot dogs, bacon.

✗ Ketchup, mayonaise.

## The Ugly

✗  Pasteries

✗  Most salad dressings.

✗  Alcohol

✗  Salt

✗  Potato chips, pretzels.

✗  Soft drinks, including diet soft drinks.

✗  Margarine

## Trans Fatty Acids

Of all of the foods that we eat none are as dangerous as those oils that have been chemically altered into trans fats. The use of high temperatures and chemicals solvents turns vegetable oils into poisonous trans fatty acids.

During the manufacturing of most margarines and shortening and other processed foods like peanut butter, pretzels, muffins, pancakes, non-dairy creamers, frosting, cake mixes, chicken nuggets etc., vegetable oils are hydrogenated or partially hydrogenated creating trans fatty acids. There have been many studies that have shown that trans fatty acids can cause heart disease, cancer and raise your bad cholesterol. Trans fatty acids are very much free radical, inflammation and acid producing foods.

## Prebiotics

The prebiotics inulin (like fertilizer in your garden or grass) and FOS are molecules of fructose and glucose that feed, nourish and increase probiotic bacteria and activity. Friendly bacteria (probiotics) help to strengthen your immune system and are essen-

tial for anyone suffering from Chronic Fatigue Syndrome, F.
myalgia, Chron's, Ulcerative Colitis, Asthma, allergies, etc. The
best prebiotic foods are garlic, bananas, barley, asparagus, onions
and tomatoes.

## Dr Martin's Best Anti-Inflammatory Foods

✓ Omega 3 – found in sardines, salmon, halibut and other cold
    water fish.

✓ Hemp seed protein, hemp seed oil and flax seed.

✓ Hot Peppers – contain capsaicin which reduces inflamma-
    tion.

✓ Celery

✓ Red grapes and red grape juice (not from concentrate).

✓ Apples

✓ Eggs – a good source of Vitamin E which helps to reduce
    inflammation.

✓ Blueberries, Raspberries, Strawberries.

✓ Extra Virgin Olive Oil

✓ Tomato sauce, watermelon, red grapefruit.

✓ Whole grains

✓ Legumes

## Pro-Inflammatory Foods

### Milk and Dairy Products – The Number One Culprit

A pediatrician friend of mine once said to me that *"milk
is highly overated."* I almost fell over when he said it. However,
the milk that we drink is hardly anything like the true milk that

existed over 50 years ago. The milk back then received no process-ing. When milk is pasterized today, sure it kills the bacteria, but, it also kills almost all of the nutritional value that milk normally contains.

"The dairy-calcium link has been firmly established in our minds by the milk industry's persuasive advertising campaigns. It's also known that the protein in dairy prod-ucts may inhibit calcium absorption." (Carl Germano, R.D., C.N.S., L.D.N., and William Cabot, M.D. – The Osteoporosis Solution)

We are often told that milk is a great source of calcium but, believe me after you heat it to 160 degrees the calcium in there is no longer absorbable. This is because the calcium has changed from organic to inorganic. The body will only use organic miner-als.

I have noticed in my practice, especially the last few years, more and more people are suffering from mucous build up due to allergies, asthma and chronic sinusitis. It amazes me that almost invariably when I take these patients off milk and dairy products their symptoms abate or almost completely disappear.

"Women who are eating dairy products to prevent osteo-porosis must pay attention to this well documented fact: The countries of the world that consume the greatest amount of dairy products also have the highest incidence of osteoporosis. The Chinese who have the lowest inci-dence of osteoporosis consume little to no cow's milk." (Harvey Diamond, Author – You Can Prevent Breast Cancer)

## Cow's Milk and Diabetes

Several studies have shown a strong association between cow's milk consumption during infancy and the later development of Type 1 (Juvenile onset) diabetes. Milk is considered a low glycemic food, which means that when you drink it, your blood sugar levels are only moderately elevated. That's the good news. Here's the bad news. When you drink milk it increases the level of insulin secreted. British researchers investigating Syndrome X, a prediabetic condition, found that women who did not drink milk were 45% less likely to develop Syndrome X. In addition, diabetes was less common among women who did not drink milk.

## Cow's Milk and Middle Ear Infections

Often I have young children in my office who suffer from recurrent middle ear infections (otitis media). The first thing that I am suspicious of is that these children are lactose intolerant. Lactose is a milk sugar that causes so many people to develop an allergy to milk. I suggest to the parents of these children that they stop giving them milk. Now, you need to understand that most parents think that if they take their children off milk, they are committing child abuse. However, I go over the fact that a cow's milk is "highly overated" and suggest to them that they substitute with "soy milk" or "rice milk". They usually listen to me. Guess what! When they stop the cow's milk – that's right – *the mucous dries up and there are no more ear infections!*

# Fruits and Vegetables Are Free Foods — Healthy Weight Loss

Friend, if you want to lose fat, eat fruits and vegetables. Fruits and vegetables are so good for you that if you snack on them frequently during the day, you will never put on a pound. As a matter of fact, fruits and vegetables help to regulate blood sugar and therefore limit the amount of insulin secreted from the pancreas. So, by eating more and more of them you will trick your fat storage mechanism in your body and you will lose fat instead of water and muscle.

# Dr. Martin's Two Day Cleanse

I want to let you in on a secret that will give you a quick start on a weight loss program. This two day program will cleanse your bowel and detoxify your system. This two day cleanse is completely safe for diabetics, hypoglycemics and people that are on any type of medication.

## For Two Days Only

Eat only fruits and vegetables and drink lots of water. Do not allow yourself to become hungry. If you allow hunger to set in your body will start to store fat. Eat as many fruits and vegetables as you like. Be creative! Homemade juices or smoothies are encouraged. This two day cleanse can be repeated every week or two times a year for spring and fall cleaning. This is excellent as an oral chelator to rid your body of heavy metals. On average my patients lose three to four pounds in two days and about 2% body fat.

## *Tips For Losing Weight*

☞ **Don't ever skip breakfast! Eat something!** – a piece of toast, fruit, egg, etc. Some women think that a good day is one when they don't eat anything until lunch. Not so. Your body's metabolism rate slows down at night and does not speed up again until you eat something. That is why it is called break-fast, you are breaking your fast. If you wait until lunch to eat, that is four or five hours that your body is burning calories at a slower rate. You are training your body to do something that you don't really want it to do. Eat something as soon as you get out of bed so that your body will begin burning calories at a faster rate until lunch.

☞ **Don't ever go more than four hours without eating**. Your body thinks you are starving so it slows down its metabolism and will even try to store the air that you breath as fat to survive. (Just kidding about the air being stored as fat, but you get my point) *Never starve yourself, never skip a meal.* Skimping can slow down the metabolism.

☞ Right after eating a meal, **immediately get up and brush your teeth, floss and mouthwash.** This makes it less appealing to want to eat more, especially before bedtime.

☞ **Chewing gum to appease hunger could work against you**. Chewing gum can have up to 15 calories per piece. The chewing gets the gastric juices going and could actually make you more hungry. The saliva that is produced while chewing goes down to the stomach, thus fooling the stomach into thinking that there is food coming soon to be digested. Drink a glass of cold water instead.

☞ **Take longer to eat your meal.** *Chew each mouthful carefully. Slow down and enjoy.* Give your brain a chance to find out that your stomach has received food. It takes 20 minutes for your stomach to tell your brain that you are full. By eating too fast you may think you want more food and pushing away from the table, thinking that you cannot eat another mouthful, is too late. You don't have to add up the calories to know that you have eaten too much.

☞ **Write down everything that you put into your mouth.** You will be surprised at how you can underestimate what you eat in one day compared to *what you actually do eat.* This is probably the downfall of any woman who is trying to lose weight.

☞ The Lord gave us a very adaptable body. **Every three days or so change what you are eating**. Your metabolism will recognize your eating routine. This is why so many women lose weight and then hit a plateau. They eat at the same time every day, and the same thing. Your metabolism doesn't know how much food you'll eat tomorrow, or the next day because those days have not happened yet. Therefore, your metabolism always burns calories based on your eating habits during the last few days because it assumes that you'll continue to eat in the same general way. So guess what! *Shock your metabolism!* Do the opposite of what it expects you to do. You are not going to eat the same type of calories and meals for more than a couple of days at a time and you will lose weight by doing this.

☞ **Trick your brain.** Instead of putting smaller portions on a big dinner plate, *put your meal on a smaller plate* so that the plate looks full! If your mind sees a full plate, it will register a full serving and you won't seem to be as hungry on smaller portions. *Eat soup with a small spoon so that it takes longer to eat.* Think of anything that will work for you personally.

☞ **Read the labels! Red alert!** Three little ingredients – high fructose corn syrup, a very common sweetener that is composed of 55% fructose and 45% glucose (Gatorade), ketchup (full of sugar), and chewing gum can sabotage your attempt to lose weight. When the back of the box or bag reads Nutrition Facts – notice the amount of calories there are for the quantity of pieces. Most bags of chips are 250 calories for 15–20 pieces of chips. Who ever stops or counts 15–20 chips? When it states calories for 125 ml – do you know how much 125 ml is? It's not very much. Most times we tend to think it is 2 or 3 times more than it actually is.

☞ **Change one habit at a time!** Those who are successful at losing weight make evolutionary changes in their diet not revolutionary changes. You have learned your eating habits over time. Change them one by one. It may not be easy, but add one healthy habit at a time and eliminate one bad health habit at a time (like skipping breakfast or eating a doughnut for breakfast).

☞ **Pick out foods beforehand** that you can snack on to feed a craving. Feed your body, not your fat cells. Be prepared, we all want our reward for being good. Or, maybe we just want something to snack on. We want something nutritious and

153

close to the comfort food that we are used to. Lets control our cravings. We can trick our brain into thinking we are succumbing to temptation. There is nothing wrong with this, it is normal. Yet, we can feel good about ourselves because we have not fallen off the wagon.

☞ **Water! Water! Water!** I know, I am not a fan of water either. However, this is the best way to flush out fat from your cells. Another added benefit is the feeling of fullness once you have finished a glass of water. Cold water is better since the body cannot use the water until it is warmed up to your body temperature. The colder the water, the more energy the body must use to warm the water, thus burning more calories.

☞ **Exercise!** The "E" word. Sorry, there is no way around this. Every time you use your muscles, you are burning fat. So keep moving. *If you don't put on your running shoes or work out clothes, its not exercise.* Buy a pedometer to keep track of how many steps you take in a day. Try to add a few more extra steps weekly. Small steps add up and helps speed up a slow metabolism. Every couple of hours do a one minute aerobic like running on the spot or jumping jacks, etc. to speed up your metabolism.

☞ **Digestive Enzymes** – If you have honestly tried your best for at least a month and there is very little weight loss then maybe you need a full spectrum digestive enzyme. Enzymes are "catalysts" or spark plugs that get other body functions started. Enzymes are involved in every process of the body. There are many different enzymes in the body and each one has a specific duty to perform. Full spectrum digestive enzymes simply means that there is the enzymes necessary to break down fats, protein, carbohydrates, fiber and milk sugar. These enzymes are considered to be pancreatic enzymes – their specific job is to digest food. To break down protein, there is Protease and Bromelain. To break down fats, there is Lipase. To break down carbohydrates, there is Amylase and Amyloglucosidase. To break down fiber, there is Cellulase, and Hemicellulase. To break down milk sugar, there is Lactase. If you are not putting out enough digestive enzymes when you eat, the body will tend to store fat much easier.

☞ **Be inventive.** Think of your own personal ways to help yourself lose weight and make it easier for yourself at the same time.

☞ **Do not be a "night time nibbler".** Night time nibbling is a guaranteed fat cell enlarger. This is when your metabolism is winding down for the day. The later at night you eat, the more of it will be stored in your cells.

## Stopping Food Cravings

✓ **Craving chocolate?** Eat a banana. It sometimes satisfies the yearning for chocolate and is much less fattening. If this doesn't work try taking a magnesium supplement. Many women are deficient in this mineral, which is found in chocolate.

✓ **Exercise!** Your appetite will temporary subside and you'll feel better.

✓ **Craving fatty foods?** Eat fish. If you are not a fish eater, then take fish oil or hemp seed oil supplements. You may be low in essential fatty acids.

✓ **Grab something to drink.** Sometimes craving for foods may be really thirst in disguise.

✓ **Sweet tooth?** Protein, fat and fiber keep blood sugar levels more even and can help keep these cravings under control.

✓ **Watch your caffeine intake.** Caffeine seems to make cravings for sugar worse.

✓ **Increase fiber intake.** This can give you more of a feeling of fullness.

✓ **Say "NO" to yourself out loud** when you are tempted to over-indulge.

**Carry a hidden picture of yourself to remind yourself of why you are trying to lose weight.**

# Chapter 7

# CHANGE #3

# Change Your Exercise

**"If we could bottle the benefits of exercise it would be the most important medication in history."**
**(William Joel Meggs, M.D., Ph.D. – The Inflammation Cure)**

## Exercise Is The One Thing You Can Do That Will:

➡ Decrease acidity in your body.

➡ Decrease free radical activity in your body.

➡ Increase energy levels.

➡ Decrease inflammation.

➡ Keep our appetite under control by reducing insulin secretion. Insulin is responsible for food cravings.

➡ Improve mental alertness and tranquility – no drug can do both at the same time but exercise can.

➡ Decrease triglycerides levels (less fat in the blood stream).

➡ Stabilizes blood sugar levels.

➡ Remove toxins from the body by stimulating the lymphatic system.

➡ Improve circulation.

➡ Benefit anti-aging.

➡ Prevent eye disease.

➡ Lower bad cholestrol.

# Built For Exercise

We were built for activity. Exercise is essential to increase energy levels, increase your pH level to alkaline, lower free radicals and decrease inflammation.

> "Ten minutes of extra activity per day can reduce an individual's risk of heart disease by 80%." (Dr. James Gavin – The Exercise Habit)

## First Problem With Exercise:

The problem with exercise is that people see it as a chore rather than pleasure. Let's get back to my twenty-one day solution. I guarantee that if you start exercising and keep at it for three weeks, you will never want to stop. If you have to write up a contract with yourself and sign it, stating that you will not quit for three weeks, no matter what happens, do it.

## Second Problem With Exercise:

The second problem that I often see is once my patients start exercising, *they go at it far too vigorously*. Of course within a few days, they are stiff and sore all over. They get discouraged and quit.

## Third Problem With Exercise:

It has been my experience that people are much more encouraged to work out in good weather. However, when winter comes they quit. This is where the third D, in the three D's comes in – *discipline*. You need to be determined to exercise 12 months of the year. Exercise has enormous benefits to your body's well being and is as important as food. You eat everyday. Therefore, you must exercise everyday. Well, not quite. The Lord made the earth in 6 days ( I always ask myself, what took him so long?), but then rested on the seventh. I think that is a good strategy. We ought to do a workout 5-6 days a week, then, *completely rest for at least one day a week.*

## Types of Exercises

➡ Weight bearing activity – walking, jogging, tennis, squash, volleyball, rollerblading, rebounding, etc.

➡ Resistance training using weights such as barbells.

➡ Core exercise

➡ Ball exercise

➡ Stretching

### Weight Bearing Activity and Aerobics

The idea here is to get moving, and more than anything else, start the release of brain hormones that will de-stress you. Remember, exercise is not exercise until you put on your running shoes. Why is this important? Study after study suggests that de-stress hormones like dopamine and serotonin are *only released when you put on your work out gear.* For example, cleaning your house or even working in the garden can be beneficial, but they are not hormone releasing exercises.

### Variety:

There is one exercise routine for everyone. Tailor one suited just for you. If you don't like jogging, don't worry about it, do something else. You need to think long-term and do everything possible to make sure you never quit.

## Here's What I Like:

As I have stated in this book already, I have been working out now for about thirty-eight years. I have found that jogging three times a week for thirty minutes, walking for fourty-five minutes once a week, and doing weight training for two days really works for me. When I jog, I run at about a five miles per hour clip. The idea is not for me to make the Olympic team, but to get a good sweat going.

## Weight Resistance Training

I really believe that resistance training should become a key component of anyone's workout regiment. Ladies, this is essential for you due to your susceptibitlty to osteoporosis. Now, once again, I am not talking about becoming a muscle bound, steroid pumping model. However, the benefits of weight resistance exercises are phenomenal.

+ **Helps prevent osteoporosis.** When muscles pull on bones, it brings more circulation and helps strengthen bone.

+ **Helps you become more flexible.** Senior citizens will greatly benefit from weight training. Older folks often have trouble getting in and out of chairs and in and out of their cars. By doing weight training for about one month, you will notice a huge improvement in movement and flexibility.

+ **Helps improve your ability to grip and open jars and lift groceries**. I've seen 80 year old patients of mine, when I put them on a weight training program, increase their strength and flexibility by a whopping 20% in 2 weeks.

## Core Exercises

Core exercises are meant to strengthen the mid-part of your body – the abdomen, low back, hips and thighs. The idea behind these exercises is to improve strength and agility in these areas. I highly recommend these type of exercise strategies for golf, old timer hockey, slow pitch baseball and other sports. Naturally, any one can benefit from core training.

## Ball Exercises

I really believe that everyone should incorporate ball exercises into their workout program. I find that by exercising on the ball you really minimize injury, especially to the low back. I like to arch my back on the ball (see diagram below) and do some sit ups before and after walking, running or lifting weights.

For those who are suffering from Chronic Fatigue and Fibromyalgia or other chronic diseases, the ball can be very beneficial to keep you agile without putting a lot of pressure on your muscles or joints.

## Stretching

Stretching exercises will help prevent injury. I find that stretching works best after you have started to sweat. I know a lot of people like to start stretching before exercising, but I found that you will get better benefits from stretching once you have warmed up. Of course, after running, walking or biking, several different stretches working all muscle groups will be beneficial.

# Chapter 8

# CHANGE #4

# Change Your Supplements

*In this chapter I will first* convince you to start taking supplements (if you don't already). If you are taking supplements, I will now convince you to start taking the right ones. Remember, there are literally thousands of supplements one can take. There are two tests that will tell you if you need to take supplements. Simply prick your finger. What color is your blood? If it is red, you need to supplement. If it is any other color, don't worry about supplements! Another test you can do to see if you need to supplement is check your address. If the last part of you address is the planet earth – you need to supplement. If the last part of your address is another planet, you don't need to supplement.

## The Four Pillars of Supplements

I believe that every man, woman, boy, and girl on the planet should be supplementing their diet with a minimum of four supplements. Now remember, it is essential that we implement the changes in our nutrition, however, *to supplement without eating properly is not wise.*

**These four supplements are the cornerstone in protecting the body against your four enemies – free radicals, inflammation, acid pH, and low energy.**

# The Four Pillars of Supplements Are:

# Antioxidants
# Essential Fatty Acids
# Enzymes
# Probiotics

## Pillar #1 – Antioxidants

Antioxidants are your body's ultimate protection against free radicals. The number one antioxidant on the market by far is Pine Bark Extract. Pine Bark Extract:

✓ **Is 50 times more powerful than Vitamin E** as an antioxidant and 20 times more powerful than Vitamin C – a powerful immune system builder.

✓ **Crosses the blood-brain barrier** – meaning that it brings extra oxygen to the brain helping to protect against Alzheimer's. By crossing the blood brain barrier it has proven to help with cognitive function (helps with short term memory, fogginess of the brain). Extra oxygen to the brain also helps with sleep disorders.

✓ **Improves micro-circulation**, therefore it is effective with:

a) diabetic retinopathy, micro-bleeding behind the eye.

b) tired or restless leg syndrome.

c) enlarged prostate

d) helps with libido.

e) increases men's sperm count.

f) helps decrease the risk of Deep Vein Thrombosis (DVT). *Make sure that you take Pine Bark Extract before you are going on a long car or plane trip.*

✓ **Is a COX inhibitor** – therefore it is effective in treating sports injuries, and arthritis.

✓ **Helps to reduce bad cholesterol.**

✓ **Is very effective in reducing platelet aggregation** which often leads to clots and heart attacks. It is as effective as aspirin, but without the side effects.

## Pine bark extract is the most powerful antioxidant.

✓ **Is a great anti-aging supplement.** Pine Bark Extract helps restore elasticity to the collagen level of the skin, making you look and feel younger. *So, you now see why I am so excited about Pine Bark Extract!*

✓ **Helps reduce inflammation.**

✓ **Helps reduce varicose veins.**

✓ **Is a natural anti-histamine** – therefore reducing asthma and allergy symptoms.

✓ **Is completely safe** – can be taken with any medication and it is water soluble.

✓ **Is bio-available.** Due to its molecular makeup, Pine Bark Extract stays in your body for up to 72 hours. Compare that with Vitamin C which has a very limited bio-availability.

✓ **Assists Vitamin C** in staying in the body longer.

Friends, have I convinced you yet? Pine Bark Extract is an essential supplement to take on a daily basis.

**Pine Bark Extract is the only product that has been clinically proven to reduce all the symptoms of Chronic Fatigue and Fibromyalgia in 6 weeks or less.**

## Not All Pine Bark Is Created Equal

There are two sources of Pine Bark Extract that have high ORAC Values. ORAC value is a measurement of antioxidant activity in any given supplement. In our commitment to excellence, we use premium quality pine bark extract in our products. You get what you pay for.

**If you are buying an inexpensive supplement, believe me, you will be finding that product in your urine, rather than in your cells.**

**Dosage:** I recommend that my patients take 25 mg. for every pound of body weight. Therefore, if your weight is 150 pounds then you will take 150 mg a day for 7-10 days. If you have a chronic disorder then take this saturation dosage for at least 6 weeks. Then take a maintenance dosage of 50-100 mg a day.

## Grape Seed Extract:

Grape Seed extract is quite good as it does a lot of things that Pine Bark Extract does, but I find that it doesn't cross the blood-brain barrier on its own.

## Other Antioxidants:

There are hundreds of antioxidants one could take including Vitamin C, Vitamin E, Beta Carotene, Selenium, Co-Enzyme Q-10. *However, the king of the hill is Pine Bark.* It has so many benefits in one capsule that taking other antioxidants is good but not essential.

### Pillar #2 – Essential Fatty Acids – Omega 3

## Hemp Seed Oil:

In my practice I recommend hemp seed oil even over fish or flax seed oils. *Hemp seed oil is the most powerful essential fatty acid that you can take.* It is nature's near perfect food.

**"Hemp seed oil is the #1 vegetable oil ahead of flax seed oil and other cold pressed edible oils."**
**(Dr. Andrew Weil)**

*Highest Source of EFA's and Best Ratio of Omega's*

➡ Alpha Linolenic Acid (ALA– Omega 3)
➡ Linolenic Acid (LA – Omega 6)

Neither of these EFA's (Essential Fatty Acids) can be synthesized by our bodies and therefore must be obtained from our diets.

A 100 gram serving of hemp seed oil contains more than 36 grams of EFA's. This is the highest amount found in any food. Hemp Seed is also 31% protein, making it second only to soybeans as a plant food source. Yet, Hemp Seed is better than soy because it contains "edestin protein," a superior protein to that found in soy. Edestin promotes protein absorption.

Hemp seed has the perfect ratio of 3:1 of Omega 6 to Omega 3 making, as nutritionists would say, an ideal nutritional balance.

## Hemp seed oil is a great anti-inflammatory because it contains one of the highest concentrations of polyunsaturated fats and the best balance of essential fatty acids.

### Medical Conditions To Use Hemp Seed Oil With:

✓ **Inflammation** – arthritis, fibromyalgia, Chron's Disease. Irritable Bowel Syndrome, etc.

✓ **Osteoporosis** – it increases calcium absorption.

✓ **Immune system** – it increases insulin function and T–Lymphocyte activity.

✓ **Energy** – it increases oxygen transportation to the cells.

✓ **Improving vitamin and mineral absorption.**

✓ **Reducing nausea symptoms** – very effective for those patients on chemotherapy.

✓ **Spastic muscles** – it has a relaxing effect.

✓ **Stimulating growth** of hair, nails, and naturally moisturizing the skin.

✔ **Reducing the risk of heart disease and stroke** by lowering cholesterol and blood pressure.

✔ **Making body fluids become more alkaline** – it contains chlorophyl which helps your body fluids to become more alkaline.

## How To Take Hemp Seed Oil:

For any type of inflammation, take 10-15 grams per day for 4 to 6 weeks. Then, take a maintenance dose of 1-2 grams per day.

## Pillar #3 – Enzymes

Enzymes act as little spark plugs in our body. They help in digesting the food that we eat. Even more so, enzymes help to make our nutrients available so that they can pass from the intestine into our blood. Enzymes in the blood take these nutrients and turn them into muscle, nerves, blood and glands.

**Enzymes help in almost every body function, especially at the cellular level. Life could not exist without them.**

We usually think of enzymes as involved only in digesting our food so that we can absorb it. We are familiar with enzymes such as:

➡ Amylase – breaks down starch

➡ Protease – breaks down protein

➡ Lipase – breaks down fat

➡ Cellulase – breaks down fiber that we get from plant foods.

Enzymes are involved in every metabolic process we have in our body. Therefore, our immune system, bloodstream, liver, kidney, spleen, and pancreas depend on enzymes.

## How Do We Get Enzymes?

➡ By eating raw food.

➡ Supplements

## Three Major Classes of Enzymes

1. **Metabolic enzymes** – they work in the blood, tissues and organs.

2. **Food enzymes** – from raw food.

3. **Digestive Enzymes** – break down the foods that we eat.

**Food processing, refining, cooking, microwaving, etc. destroys the enzymes in our food.**

## Systemic Oral Enzymes – The New Kid On The Block

There is strong evidence that by taking digestive enzymes like Amylase, Protease, Cellulase and Lipase in a supplement form could help in reducing inflammation in the body. This is besides being quite good in helping with digestion. There are over 100 studies that have shown the benefits of enzyme therapy in treating sports injuries, arthritis and other inflammatory conditions. Systemic Oral Enzymes:

✔ Help reduce swelling in the joints, muscles and soft tissue.

✓  Help to repair ligaments, joints, and cartilage.

✓  Are of great benefit to those suffering from rheumatoid arthritis, osteoarthritis, fibromyalgia and sports injuries.

✓  Reduce inflammation in arteries and blood vessels.

## The Problem With Enzymes

Enzymes, like I have said, are great for digestion, however, they are quite susceptible to breaking down in the stomach due to high acidity. Therefore, to get any anti-inflammatory results doctors would have to prescribe massive dosages of enzymes. This was to ensure that some of the enzymes will make it into the bloodstream. Another trick that was tried was to coat these enzymes several times in the hope that they can pass the stomach's acidity. However, it took so much enteric coating that most tablets couldn't be dissolved in the small intestine.

## The Solution:

The solution of getting the enzymes into the blood stream has now been solved. Fungus based enzymes break down at a much different pH. Thus, *they go directly into the bloodstream* and look for any site of inflammation in the body. They act like pacmen breaking down fibrin (a little substance that can lead to scar tissue in joints and muscle).

*For more information on how to order Systemic Oral Enzymes visit our website at www.martinnutra.com or call 1–866–365–6868.*

## Pillar #4 – Probiotics

Another cornerstone supplement that everyone needs to take are called Probiotics, or friendly bacteria. The lining of our bowel is made up of several thousand kinds of different bacteria. They are called friendly bacteria because these little guys are on our side. These friendly bacteria are known to play an important role in preventing disease.

> "Our overuse of medical antibiotics has reduced the human gut to a burned–out minefield destroying the good guys along with the bad guys." (Jordan S. Rubin – The Maker's Diet)

### Not Only The Bowel

Another important thing that the researchers have been finding out that friendly bacteria is lining our bowel, but they are also anywhere you have mucous membranes, such as in the sinuses, esophagus, lungs and reproductive organs.

### What Kills These Friendly Bacteria?

The number one cause of destruction of these little critters is the overuse of antibiotics. Farmers use them to cut down on infections in their poultry, cattle and pigs.

Remember, antiobiotics don't know what to kill, so they attack the bad guys as well as the good guys. The problem with that, friendly bacteria are our primary defense in protecting us against foreign invaders. The overuse of antibiotics kills friendly bacteria and makes us much more susceptible to chronic diseases like Chronic Fatigue Syndrome. Our population, in general, is much less healthy. We see all the new diseases and super-bugs coming because of the overuse of antibiotics.

**It is estimated that U.S. pharmaceutical companies alone produce over 35 million pounds of antibiotics each year. Animals receive the majority of them.**

## Yeast and Parasite Infections

Another huge problem that develops with antibiotics is that the bowel is stripped of its natural friendly bacteria. When this happens, yeast, fungus, and parasites can easily move through the intestines into the bloodstream.

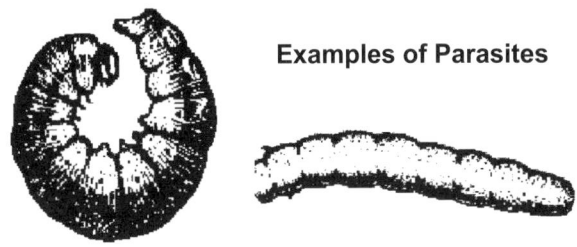

**Examples of Parasites**

## Mycotoxins In The Blood

When mycotoxins (parasites, yeast, fungus and their droppings) get into the blood they love to set up shop and start having a family. White blood cells which look out for viruses and bacteria rarely react to the invasion of yeast, fungus or parasites. These microscopic bugs toxify our bodies, deplete the immune system, acidify our blood's pH and set up an inflammatory response in our bodies.

When I analyze blood, I rarely see an exception to this equation:

---
**Antiobiotics = Yeast / Fungus / Parasitic infection in the blood**
---

## What Else Kills Our Friendly Bacteria?

➡ **Drinking water with chlorine** – almost every major city and town in the U.S. and Canada uses chlorine in their water to kill germs.

➡ **The Cleanliness Syndrome** – We are so bent on keeping our selves clean that we are destroying lots of freindly bacteria at the same time. Research in the 80's and 90's showed that children who came from larger families were less likely to develop asthma, hay fever, and eczema. Why? Because mom didn't have the time to worry about over cleaning her kids.

My wife and I come from two very different family backgrounds. Rose-Marie was an only child and her mother kept her spotless all day long when she was a little girl. How do I know? My mother-in-law was constantly after our four kids to wash their hands, cleaning their face with an ever present face cloth, baths morning and night – clean, clean, clean. Now I came from a family of 11 children. Do you think that my mom had time to inspect the kids for cleanliness, or follow them around with a face cloth? It's also true that Rose-Marie had every infection known to man as a young child and later developed Chronic Fatigue Syndrome. Just a coincidence?

Now folks, I am not saying not to wash your hands. What I am saying is that we have become a paranoid society terrified of germs. *Germs don't cause disease – a poor immune system is the problem.*

## Hospitals

Do you know where the worst place for germs is in the whole wide world? You probably would have never guessed – *our hospitals!* Hospitals are the worst because they clean and disinfect so much that they have stripped away bacteria including the friendly ones.

You know what happens? Virulent bacteria like C-Difficile waltzes into hospitals and creates havoc with compromised immune systems because there is no friendly bacteria to counter act their effects.

## Where Do You Get Friendly Bacteria?

✔ **Work in the garden**. Some of those friendly bacteria will get into your system.

✔ **Eat yogurt.** The problem with most yogurts is that they contain few bacteria strains.

✔ **Go to the health food store.** Pick up probiotics in the refrigerator at you local health food store. Remember, probiotics have many different bacterial strands and different bacterial strands go to different places in the body. You need to be protected from your sinuses to reproductive organs. So just taking one strand like Acidophilus for example is not enough.

Don't get excited when you read the label. There are five billion friendly bacteria in each capsule. Like I said, it is more important that you see how many different strands are available in the name brand that you are buying.

## Prebiotics

Prebiotics are fertilizer for friendly bacteria. Remember, these little friendly bacteria need to be fed once they are in your body. Bananas, tomatoes, garlic, barley, asparagus and onions are great food for friendly bacteria.

**These foods act like fertilizers for the friendly bacteria.**

## The Four Pillars of Supplements

There are thousands of supplements that we can take. However, for giving your body the best health foundation use:

✓ **Pine Bark Extract** – antioxidant
✓ **Hemp Seed Oil** – essential fatty acid
✓ **Enzymes**
✓ **Probiotics**

If you take these four supplements you will give your body what it needs to survive in this world in which we live.

# Chapter 9

# Chronic Fatigue Syndrome and Fibromyalgia

## THE MODERN DAY CURSE

*You know the best lessons* in life are usually the lessons we learn through adversity. When the storms of life come (and they will) I really try and find out what God is trying to teach me. I find that when my resources are depleted, I rely on God even more. I say this to tell you that I really became more interested in finding out about Chronic Fatigue and Fibromyalgia after my dear wife Rose-Marie was affected with this condition in 1991.

> "Whatever I have, wherever I am, I can make it through anything in the One who makes me who I am." (Philippians 4:13, The Message™ – The Bible in Contemporary Language, Eugene Peterson)

Our life *changed drastically* around our house when this once super-mom could no longer function on a day-to-day basis. But, you know as I look back on the last 15 years of watching my wife live with this disease, I am amazed at how much God has taught me. As I write this book, I thank the Lord for giving me a heart and compassion for people suffering from chronic illnesses. You know God can use that when it hits close to home. As the apostle Paul said in his letter to the Romans "That's why we can be so sure that every detail in our lives is worked into something good" (Romans 8:28, The Message™ – The Bible in Contemporary Language, Eugene Peterson).

# Steps To Fight Chronic Fatigue Syndrome For The Modern Woman

The book "Steps To Fight Chronic Fatigue Syndrome For The Modern Woman" came to fruition in 1999 after I finally reached an understanding of the cause of Chronic Fatigue Syndrome and Fibromyalgia. My wife (God bless her) became my guinea pig. I tried every test and treatment plan to try and tackle this major problem in her life and thousands of patients also.

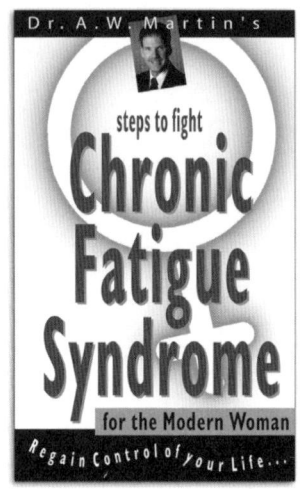

## Here Is What I Discovered:

### The Cause:

After listening to literally thousands of patients who suffer from Chronic Fatigue Syndrome I came to these conclusions:

➡ Chronic Fatigue and Fibromyalgia is a modern day dilemma. For those who say that there is nothing new under the sun, I remind them of AIDS. Do you know that there was no such thing as AIDS before the late 70's? AIDS wasn't even in our texbooks. How about autism? Did you know that 1 out of 166 children born today in the Western world has autism. Folks, I never heard of autism until 1980.

➡ Chronic Fatigue Syndrome and Fibromyalgia patients have consistently been exposed to a combination of one or more of the following precursors that deplete the function of their immune system and adrenal glands:

a) **Long history of antibiotic use** – either for recurrent middle ear, tonsils, bladder or urinary tract infections or for the treatment of acne.

b) **High stress situation** – typical Type A personality, very motivated, often a perfectionist, trying to be a super-mom while holding down a job outside of the home.

c) **Use of birth control pill** – usually for more than two years.

d) **Tight House Syndrome** – R2000 homes have very little air exchange.

e) **Toxic Building Syndrome** – exposure to mold, pollution or chemicals at work.

f) **Poor nutrition** – far too many fast foods.
– very low amount of fruits and vegetables
– too much caffeine
– too many simple carbohydrates such as sugar, pastries, muffins, bagels etc.

g) **Trauma** – often a simple car accident or loss of a loved one would be the straw that broke the camel's back.

h) **Chemicals in the home** – The overuse of chemical household cleaners, air fresheners, shampoos and deodorants.

**"My experience has shown Fibromyalgia patients usually have three or four major nutritional deficiencies along with a low antioxidant level."**
(Dr. Ray D.S. Strand M.D., Fibromyalgia)

# Adrenal Gland Exhaustion

*Adrenal gland exhaustion is the number one physiological factor in Chronic Fatigue Syndrome and Fibromyalgia.* The adrenal glands curve over the top of each kidney in the abdomen. They secrete key stress hormones such as, cortisol, DHEA and adrenaline. In Chronic Fatigue sufferers, these hormones are often at abnormal levels. This is called the continuous stress response. These hormones can influence a number of body functions, from immune response to the kind of sleep that we get at night. With the abnormal secretions of hormones, fatigue and muscle pain may result.

When the modern day woman (and some men) are bombarded with continuous stress, both externally and internally, these little stress glands become exhausted. When this occurs it sets off a borage of other symptoms.

**Overtaxed adrenal glands are responsible for a number of symptoms that the chronic fatigue and fibromyalgia patient experiences.**

# The Four Major Symptoms

**❶ Onset of debilitating fatigue** that lasts for more than 6 weeks.

**❷ Cognitive** means brain function. Chronic Fatigue Syndrome and Fibromyalgia patients usually complain of:
a) decrease in short term memory
b) fogginess of the brain – difficulty in concentrating

❸ **Sleep disorder** – even though these patients are exhausted they suffered from poor sleep which often include sleep apnea and poor recuperative sleep.

❹ **Fibromyalgia Symptoms** – Fibromyalgia could be characterized as an *"arthritis of the muscles"* with symptoms of burning type pain in muscles of the neck, mid and low back, face and legs. This type of pain was so severe that most pain medication proved to be useless.

## I have found that over 95% of Chronic Fatigue Syndrome patients suffer from Fibromyalgia.

Chronic Fatigue and Fibromyalgia patients almost always had several or all of these other symptoms or conditions:

➡ **Decrease in metabolic rate** – most Chronic Fatigue and Fibromyalgia patients suffer from a low thyroid function. Again, thyroid readings were within normal limits in most cases but, the TSH (Thyroid Stimulating Hormone) readings were in the lower number of normal.

➡ **Low blood sugar** – Functional Hypoglycemia

| Pathological Hypoglycemia | Functional Hypoglycemia |
|---|---|
| Fasting blood sugar level can be 2.2 | Blood sugar never gets as low as 2.2 |
| Blood sugar is affected by fasting and meals | Blood sugar dips at different times of the day |

➡ **Onset or worsening of allergy symptoms** – environmental, chemical and food allergies.

➡ **Leaky Gut Syndrome** or Irritable Bowel Syndrome (IBS).

"NSAID's like Tylenol, Motrin, Advil, and dozens of others are gentler on the stomach lining but, they are much more irritating to the intestinal lining. They cause damage to the lining by blocking prostaglandins that stimulate repair. They are a direct cause of leaky gut syndrome, food sensitivities and inflammatory problems like arthritis and eczema." (Elizabeth Lipski, M.S., C.C.N. – Digestive Wellness)

## Testing

Here at the Martin Clinic we have developed a protocol of testing our patients suffering from fatigue. Without exception we have found that people have four different findings:

❶ **Severe Rouleaux Formation of Their Red Blood Cells** – This was a major factor in the patient's fatigue, mainly because there is poor oxygen and nutritional delivery plus poor waste expulsion due to red blood cell clumping.

❷ **Very Acidic pH** – An acidic pH is corrosive on the cells and makes the body much more susceptible to viral, bacterial, fungal and yeast proliferation in the body.

❸ **High Amounts of Free Radicals** – Urine tests and live blood cell analysis would demonstrate severe "rusting out" of the patient's cells.

❹ **Inflammation Response** – These patients had a chronic inflammation hormone in the body. I believe this was due to adrenal gland burnout and the loss of normal levels of the anti-inflammatory in hormones in the body called cortisol.

## Lymph System — The Heart and Soul of The Body's Defense Mechanism

The lymph system is the sewage system to your blood stream. The lymph system is made of fluid, organs, nodes, ducts, glands and vessels that continuously cleanse the body of "crap" or waste. The lymphatic system contains three times more fluid in your body than blood. What does that tell you about how important it is? However, unlike the circulatory system, the lympathic system only carries away fluid from the tissues. It picks up waste from all the cells and arranges their elimination from the body. They also produce white blood cells which are like "pacmen" that go throughout the body looking for foreign invaders (bad guys) such as bacteria and viruses, then removes them from the body as well. It is essential that people who suffer from Chronic Fatigue, Fibromyalgia, Rheumatoid Arthritis, or any other chronic disease understand that if they do nothing else they must get the lymphatic system draining. With this in mind I have put together a easy to do lymphatic drainage exercise program.

## Lymphatic Drainage Exercise Program
### Exercise For Those Who Can't

Note: Purchase a BIG exercise ball. The bigger, the better! You will find it easier than using a small ball.

### Figure A – Full Arch

Arch back over the ball as far back as possible. Stay in this position for 10 seconds.

### Figure B – Stimulates The Thymus Gland

Lay back over the ball with arms extended. Lift head and count to three.

Repeat 5-10 times.

### Figure C – Lateral Stretch

Lie sideways on the ball and cup back of head. Lift head and shoulders.

### Figure D – Lumbar Stretch

Lay on stomach over the ball. Cross your arms over the ball and arch back.

Count to three and repeat 5 times.

### Figure E

Using light weights (2 to 5 pounds) arch back over the ball and extend arms with weight.

Great for the abs and prevention of hernias.

## Figure F & G

Using light weights, lay flat on the ball.

Make sure that your head rests on the ball.

Extend arms vertically.

Repeat 10-15 times.

Great for chest muscles and lymphatic drainage in the arms.

## Figure H

Using light weights, kneel (if possible) behind the ball. Flex arm vertically.

Repeat 10-15 times then switch arms.

## Figure I

While sitting on the ball, with light weights, start with both arms bent at the elbows at shoulder level. Push weights up. Repeat 10-15 times.

Great for shoulder exercise.

## Figure J

While sitting on the ball, using both arms, bring both weights at the same time over the back of your head.

Repeat 10–15 times.

Great triceps and lymphatic drainage.

# Synopsis of What Happens In A Typical CFS and Fibromyalgia Patient

## Step 1:

Combination of exposure to one or more of the following:

- Antibiotics
- Stress
- Birth control pills
- Tight House Syndrome
- Environmental sensitivies (mold, pollution, etc.)
- Trauma (i.e. car accident)
- Poor nutrition
- Cleaning with household chemicals
- Chemicals in personal hygiene products

## Step 2:

Adrenal Gland exhaustion resulting in:

- Commencement of fatigue
- Hypoglycemia
- Low blood pressure
- Poor immune system function
- Allergies
- Repeated infections (bladder, ear)
- Respiratory infections
- Fibromyalgia symptoms due to low secretion of cortisol

## Step 3:

- Inflammation response
- Change in red blood cell structure
- Increase in free radical damage
- Acidic pH

## Step 4:

- Brain swelling
- Decreased blood flow and oxygen supply to the brain
- Suppressed Hypothalamus – the orchestra leader of the following glands:

| Suppressed Thyroid | Suppressed Pineal Gland | Suppressed Pituitary Gland | Ovaries |
|---|---|---|---|
| Fatigue, lower blood pressure, always cold, irregular heartbeats | Decrease in melatonin production | Weakness | PMS |
| Decreased basal metabolic rate | Sleep disorder | Decrease in libido | Menstrual cycle disorder |

# References

## Introduction & Chapter 1

Beauchesne, Eric. Middle Age Stress Hits Woman Hard at Work, National Post, August 31, 2005.

Dadd, Debra Lynn. Home Safe Home, Putnam Publishing Group, 1997.

Denk, Steve. Clinical Microscopy and Blood Cell Analysis, Biomedx.com.

Diamond, Harvey. You Can Prevent Breast Cancer, ProMotion Publishing, San Diego, California.

Graci, Sam. The Path to Phenomenal Health, Wiley, 2005.

MacKenzie, Karen. Children and Chemical Exposure Outside the Home, RM Barry Publications, 2005.

Martin, A. W. La Fibromyalgie et le Syndrome de la Fatigue Chronique, Les Editions, Quebecor, 1999.

Martin, A. W. Sugar: Be Informed, Healthwatch, R&T Press, Vol. 1, Issue 10.

McCasland, David. Our Daily Bread, May 3, 2006.

McDougall John, M.D. McDougall's Medicine: A Challenging Second Opinion; New Century, 1985.

Schmidt, M. Tired of Being Tired – Overcoming Chronic Fatigue Syndrome Epidemic and Low Energy, Frog Limited, Berkley, California, 1995.

## Chapter 2

Barefoort, Robert, and Reich, Carl J. M.D. The Calcium Factor – 2nd Edition (revised), Bokar Consultants, 1996.

Denk, Steve. Clinical Microscopy, Biomedx.com.

Graci, Sam. The Path to Phenomenal Health, Wiley, 2005.

Lipsky, Elizabeth. Digestive Wellness – 2nd Edition, Keats Publishing, 1996.

Rubin, Jordan S. The Maker's Diet, The Berkley Publishing Group, 2004.

## Chapter 3

Cooper, Kenneth, H. The Antioxidant Revolution, Thomas Nelson Publishers, 1994.

Challem, Jack. The Nutrition Reporter, May 2000, Vol.11, #5.

Facchini, F.S., Humphreys, M.H., Donasamento, Ca, et al. Relation between insulin resistance and plasma concentrations of lipid Hydroproxide, Carotenoids and Tocopherols, American Journal of Clinical Nutrition, 72:776-779, 2000.

Guthrie, Catherine. The Anti-Inflammatory Diet, Alternative Medicine, November/December 2003.

Martin, A. W. Steps To Fight Chronic Fatigue Syndrome For The Modern Woman, R&T Press, 1999.

Passwater, R. The New Superantioxidant Plus, Keats Publishing, 1992.

Simon, J. Antioxidants and Their Effects, The American Chiropractor, March/April 1995.

Pero, Ronald, and Zimmerman, Marcia. Reverse Aging, Nutrition Solution Publications, 2002.

Ullegaddi, R, et al. European Journal of Clinical Nutrition, 59:1367-1373, 2005.

# Chapter 4

Alexander, R. Top 10 Harardous Household Cleaners, The Consumer Law Page.

Bielski, Zosia. Taking Measure, National Post, March 15, 2006.

Challem, Jack. The Nutrition Reporter, Vol. 11, Issue 9, September 2000.

Challem, Jack. The Nutrition Reporter, Vol. 16, Issue 10, October 2005.

Davis, Gary, and Turner, E. Safe Substitutes at Home, Non-Toxic Products, University of Tennessee.

Kirkey, Sharon. Canadian Research Says Bye to BMI, National Post, March 15, 2006.

Kolata, Gina. A Protein Linked To Heart Attacks, Toronto Star, January 7, 2005.

Meggs, William Joel. The Inflammation Cure, McGraw Hill, 2004.

Templin, Bunda. Household Toxics, RM Barry Publications, 2005.

Underwood, Anne. Quieting A Body's Defenses, Newsweek, Summer 2005.

# Chapter 5

Martin, A. W. The New Thin You, R&T Press, 1998.

# Chapter 6

Ballentine, R. Diet and Nutrition, a holistic approach, Himalayan Publishers, 1978.

Challem, J. VITE and Other Micronutrients Reduce Diabetic Complications and Insulin Resistance, The Nutrition Reporter, Vol. 8, Issue 3, March 1997.

Challem, J. Most People Still Not Eating Fruits and Veggies, The Nutrition Reporter, Vol. 11, Issue 10.

Challem, J. Resveratrol Might Fight Influenza Germs, The Nutrition Reporter, Vol. 16, Issue 10.

Challem, J. Avoiding Milk May Lower Diabetes Risk, The Nutrition Reporter, Vol. 16, Issue 10.

Challem, J. Red Delicious Apples with Skin Contain Potent Antioxidant Levels, The Nutrition Reporter, Vol. 11, Issue 9.

Challem, J. Cow's Milk Increases Diabetes Risk in Children, The Nutrition Reporter, Vol. 11, Issue 9.

Challem, J. Lycopene – An Antioxidant Found In Tomatoes, The Nutrition Reporter, Vol. 14, Issue 9, September 2003.

Challem, J. Eating Fish Benefits Older Hearts, The Nutrition Reporter, Vol. 12, Issue 5, May 2001.

Challem, J. Researchers Identify Anti-Inflammatory Constituent In Extra Virgin Olive Oil, The Nutrition Reporter, Vol. 16, Issue 1, November 2005.

Challem, J. Eating Eggs Instead of Bagels For Breakfast Leaves You Less Hungry, The Nutrition Reporter, Vol. 17, Issue 3, March 2006.

Challem, J. Pycnogenol Has Anti-Inflammatory Properties, The Nutrition Reporter, Vol. 12, Issue 1, January 2001.

Challem, J. Omega 3 Fatty Acids Reduce Pain, The Nutrition Reporter, Vol. 14, Issue 9, September 2003.

Heinerman, J. Heinerman's New Encyclopedia of Fruits and Vegetables, Reward Books, Parker Publishing Company, 1995.

Martin, A. W. Steps To Fight Chronic Fatigue Syndrome For The Modern Woman, R&T Press, 1999.

Martin, A. W., and Martin, A. P. Joint-Zyme: The Future of Natural Therapy, Team Writers Group, 2002.

Martin, A. W. Pycnogenol – The Bark With The Bite, R&T Press, 1998.

Quillin, P. Healing Secrets From The Bible, The Leader Company Inc., 1998.

Reader's Digest. Foods That Harm, Foods That Heal, 1996.

## Chapter 7

Cooper, Kenneth. The Antioxidant Revolution, Thomas Nelson Publishers, 1994.

Martin, A. W. The New Thin You, R&T Press, 1998.

## Chapter 8

Elkins, Rita. Digestive Enzymes, Woodland Publishing, 1998.

Martin, A. W., and Martin, A. P. Joint-Zyme – The Future of Natural Therapy, Team Writers Group, 2002.

Martin, A. W. Steps To Fight Chronic Fatigue Syndrome, Free Radical Damage and Pycnogenol, Lasalle University, 1997.

Passwater, R. The New Superantioxidant Plus, Keats Publishing, 1992.

Rona, Z. Health Wise Digest, Issue 10, February 2001.

Rubin, Jordan S. The Maker's Diet, The Berkley Publishing Group, 2004.

## Chapter 9

Ali, M. The Canary and Chronic Fatigue, Lifespan Press, 1995.

Goldberg, B. Chronic Fatigue, Fibromyalgia and Environmental Illness, Future Medicine Publishing, 1998.

Martin, A. W. Chronic Fatigue Syndrome, Free Radical Damage and Pycnogenol, Lasalle University, 1997.

Martin, A. W. Steps To Fight Chronic Fatigue Syndrome For The Modern Woman, R&T Press, 1999.

Ostrum, N. 50 Things You Should Know About The Chronic Fatigue Syndrome Epidemic, St. Martin's Paperbacks, 1993.

Rosenbaum, M, and Susser, M. Solving The Puzzle of Chronic Fatigue Syndrome, Life Sciences Press, 1992.

Schmidt, M. Tired of Being Tired – Overcoming Chronic Fatigue Syndrome Epidemic and Low Energy, Frog Limited, Berkley, California, 1995.

Teitelbaum, J. From Fatigued to Fantastic, Avery Publishing, 1996.